Top 25 locator map
(continues on inside
back cover)
◄

CityPack
Berlin *Top 25*

**CHRISTOPHER AND
MELANIE RICE**

AA Publishing
Find out more about AA Publishing
and the wide range of services the AA
provides by visiting our website at
www.theAA.com/bookshop

If you have any comments
or suggestions for this guide
you can contact the editor at
Citypack@theAA.com

About This Book

KEY TO SYMBOLS

✚ Map reference to the accompanying fold-out map and Top 25 locator map

✉ Address

☎ Telephone number

🕐 Opening/closing times

🍴 Restaurant or café on premises or nearby

🚉 Nearest railway station

🚇 Nearest subway (tube) station

🚌 Nearest bus route

⛴ Nearest riverboat or ferry stop

♿ Facilities for visitors with disabilities

✋ Admission charges: Expensive (over €5), Moderate (€2.5–€5), and Inexpensive (under €2.5).

↔ Other nearby places of interest

❓ Other practical information

▶ Indicates the page where you will find a fuller description

ℹ Tourist information

ORGANIZATION

This guide is divided into six chapters:
- Planning Ahead, Getting There
- Living Berlin—Berlin Now, Berlin Then, Time to Shop, Out and About, Walks, Berlin by Night
- Berlin's Top 25 Sights
- Berlin's Best—best of the rest
- Where To—detailed listings of restaurants, hotels, shops and nightlife
- Travel Facts—practical information

In addition, easy-to-read side panels provide extra facts and snippets, highlights of places to visit and invaluable practical advice.

The colours of the tabs on the page corners match the colours of the triangles aligned with the chapter names on the contents page opposite.

MAPS

The fold-out map in the wallet at the back of this book is a comprehensive street plan of Berlin. The first (or only) grid reference given for each attraction refers to this map. **The Top 25 locator map** found on the inside front and back covers of the book itself is for quick reference. It shows the Top 25 Sights, described on pages 26–50, which are clearly plotted by number (**1**–**25**, not page number) across the city. The second map reference given for the Top 25 Sights refers to this map.

Contents

PLANNING AHEAD, GETTING THERE   4 – 7

LIVING BERLIN   8 – 24

BERLIN'S TOP 25 SIGHTS   25 – 50

1 Sanssouci *26*
2 Cecilienhof *27*
3 Klein-Glienicke *28*
4 Spandau Zitadelle *29*
5 Jagdschloss Grunewald *30*
6 Sachsenhausen *31*
7 Ethnologisches Museum *32*
8 Schloss Charlottenburg *33*
9 Kurfürstendamm *34*
10 Kaiser-Wilhelm-Gedächtniskirche *35*
11 Bauhaus-Archiv *36*
12 Kulturforum *37*
13 Kunstgewerbemuseum *38*
14 Tiergarten *39*
15 Potsdamer Platz *40*

16 Brandenburger Tor *41*
17 Checkpoint Charlie *42*
18 Gendarmenmarkt *43*
19 Unter den Linden *44*
20 Museumsinsel *45*
21 Pergamon Museum *46*
22 Berliner Dom *47*
23 Nikolaiviertel *48*
24 Alexanderplatz *49*
25 Schloss Köpenick *50*

BERLIN'S BEST   51 – 62

WHERE TO   63 – 88

TRAVEL FACTS   89 – 93

INDEX   94 – 95

CREDITS AND ACKNOWLEDGEMENTS   96

Planning Ahead

WHEN TO GO

Expect some rain at any time, and the possibility of hot and humid weather in summer. April to June is the most comfortable period to vist. The arts scene is liveliest between October and May. From the end of November up to Christmas the city is lit up with decorations and the streets are filled with markets.

TIME

Berlin is one hour ahead of the UK, six hours ahead of New York, and nine hours ahead of Los Angeles.

AVERAGE DAILY MAXIMUM TEMPERATURES

JAN	FEB	MAR	APR	MAY	JUN	JUL	AUG	SEP	OCT	NOV	DEC
35°F	39°F	47°F	54°F	65°F	70°F	73°F	73°F	66°F	56°F	45°F	38°F
1°C	3°C	8°C	12°C	18°C	21°C	22°C	22°C	18°C	13°C	7°C	3°C

Spring (mid-March to end–May) is extremely pleasant, with flowers and trees coming into bloom throughout the parks and along the avenues.

Summer (June to early September) can be hot with the occasional dramatic thunder storm.

Autumn (mid-September to end–November) is comfortable, but changeable with fine bright weather often preceded by periods of drizzle and grey skies.

Winter (December to mid-March) is extremely cold with occasional snowfalls, but it is common to experience crisp, bright days.

WHAT'S ON

On any given day, Berlin has around 250 exhibitions and more than 400 independent theatre groups, 170 museums, 200 art galleries and 150 auditoriums. For details of listings magazines ► 24.

January *6-Day Race*: Cycling event at the Velodrom, Landsberger Allee.

February *International Film Festival (Berlinale)*: The world's filmmakers come to Potsdamer Platz.

May *German Women's Open*: Tennis tournament.

June *Fête de la Musique*:

Concerts (from rock to classical) at Brandenburg Gate, Hackesche Höfe and other open-air venues. *Christopher Street Day*: Gay and lesbian procession.

July *Love Parade*: 'The largest rave party in the world'. Involving 1.5 million young people. Strasse des 17 Juni, Tiergarten.

August *Lange Nacht der Museen:* Over 100 museums are open after midnight.

September *Berliner Festwochen*: A month of opera, music, theatre and painting throughout the city.

September/October *Berlin Marathon*.

October *German Unity Day* (3 Oct): Street festivals on Unter den Linden.

November *Jazz Festival Berlin*: Jazz concerts are held citywide.

December *Christmas Markets*: All month at Opernpalais (Unter den Linden 5), Breitscheidplatz, Alexanderplatz, Winterfeldtplatz (Sundays only) and Spandau Altstadt. *New Year*: Celebrations at the Brandenburg Gate and a gala evening at Staatsoper.

BERLIN ONLINE

www.berlin-tourist-information.de
The official site for the Berlin tourist board with details of hotels, sightseeing, guided tours and current events. You can also order theatre and concert tickets online and make hotel bookings from their list of approved hotels. In English and German.

www.berlin.de
The city of Berlin's official site with details of all the current events in both English and German.

www.berlinOnline.de
A site providing information on life in the city from the latest news and jobs to current events, clubbing, shopping and ticket information. In German only.

www.meinberlin.de
A German-only site focusing on the cultural and leisure activities in Berlin.

www.freshmilk.de
A creative site in German only dedicated to multimedia, modern art and culture from video and cinema to music and exhibitions.

www.tip-berlin.de
The official German language site for the listings magazine *Tip*, detailing the major events and what is going on in the capital in the way of films, music and partying in the month ahead.

www.zitty.de
In German only, the official site for the listings magazine *Zitty*, reviewing the top films, restaurants and bars in Berlin.

www.taz.de
The site of Berlin newspaper *Das Tagesspiegel*, in German, with all the latest news and views.

www.bvg.de
Useful site in English and German giving detailed information on travelling around the city.

GOOD TRAVEL SITES

www.fodors.com
A complete travel-planning site. You can research prices and weather; book air tickets, cars and rooms; ask questions (and get answers) from fellow travellers; and find links to other sites.

www.tripadvisor.com
Promises unbiased reviews and recommendations of hotels, resorts, vacations and guides and lists the top attractions and hotels in major cities across the globe.

CYBERCAFÉS

easyInternetCafé
⊞ E7
✉ Kurfürstendamm 224
☎ 030 88 70 79 70
🕐 24 hours
🚇 U-Kurfürstendamm

Netz-Werk
⊞ Off map
✉ Sonntagstrassse 6
☎ 030 29 49 06 54
🕐 12–5
🚇 S-Bahn Ostkreuz

Surf and Sushi
⊞ J4 ✉ Oranienburger Strasse 17
☎ 030 28 38 48 98
🕐 12–late
🚇 S-Bahn Hackescher Markt

Getting There

ENTRY REQUIREMENTS

EU nationals need a valid national identity card or passport, valid for at least six months. Citizens of the US, Canada, Australia and New Zealand need a passport, valid for at least six months, for stays of up to three months. Citizens of other countries should check visa requirements with the German Embassy.

MONEY

Germany's currency is the euro (€). Notes come in denominations of 5, 10, 20, 50, 100, 200, and 500 euros, and coins in denominations of 1, 2, 5, 10, 20, and 50 cents, and 1 and 2 euros.

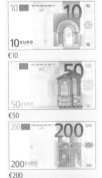

€10

€50

€200

€500

ARRIVING

Berlin has three international airports: Tegel, 8km (5 miles) to the northwest of central Berlin; Schönefeld, 18km (11 miles) to the southeast; and Tempelhof, 4km (2.5 miles) to the south. Tempelhof handles all domestic and charter flights.

ARRIVING AT TEGEL AIRPORT

✚ B1. For airport information ☎ 0180 500 0186. The airport is linked to the city via the bus network. Bus 109 from the airport will take you to Zoo Station and bus X9 goes to the Kurfürstendamm (30 min). Bus 128 goes to the north of Berlin, while the TXL bus goes as far as the government district. A taxi right into the city costs around €17 and takes around 20 minutes.

ARRIVING AT SCHÖNEFELD AIRPORT

✚ Off map. For airport information ☎ 0180 500 0186. There is a free shuttle transfer from the terminal building to Berlin-Schönefeld airport station. The Airport Express takes passengers from the airport to the Kurfürstendamm (30 min). The 171 bus links the terminal building with the Rudow U-Bahn station and the U7 line. A taxi to the heart of the city costs around €30 and takes around 40 minutes.

ARRIVING AT TEMPELHOF AIRPORT

✚ J9. For airport information ☎ 030 69 51 22 88. Direct U-Bahn links between Platz der Luftbrücke station at the airport mean that you can reach the heart of the city in 10–20 minutes. Take the U-Bahn line 6 from Platz der Luftbrücke (*not* Tempelhof) into the city. Change at Friedrichstrasse for the western side of the city. A taxi to central Berlin costs around €15 and takes around 15 minutes.

Arriving by Bus
Berlin's central bus station (ZOB) is on Masurenallee opposite the International Conference Centre (ICC) in the district of Charlottenburg. For travel information ☎ 030 302 53 61/030 30 10 01 75 (24 hour). For tickets call 030 301 03 80 (Mon–Fri 6–7.30, Sat–Sun 6–3).

Arriving by Train
There are good connections from Paris, Brussels, Copenhagen, Warsaw, Moscow, Vienna and Prague. The main stations are Berlin-Lichtenberg and Zoo Station (Bahnhof Zoo). For train information: Deutsche Bahn AG (German National Railway) ✚ E6 ✉ Hardenbergplatz 11 ☎ 11 8 61 (24 hour), www.bahn.de.

Arriving by Car
A ring road provides access from the north and south and southern and eastern road links are currently being improved and modernized. If you intend to bring your car into Central Berlin, find a hotel with parking as there are few car parks and little on-street parking.

Getting Around
Before taking the U-Bahn (underground) and S-Bahn (city railway) you must first buy a valid ticket from station foyers or from vending machines on platforms. Routes are referred to by the final stop on the line. You must validate your ticket at a machine on the platform before boarding the train. Enter cream double-decker buses at the front and leave by the doors in the middle or at the back. Pay the driver with small change or show a valid ticket.

For more information on getting around ➤ 91.

Living
Berlin

Berlin Now *10–15*

Berlin Then *16–17*

Time to Shop *18–19*

Out and About *20–21*

Walks *22–23*

Berlin by Night *24*

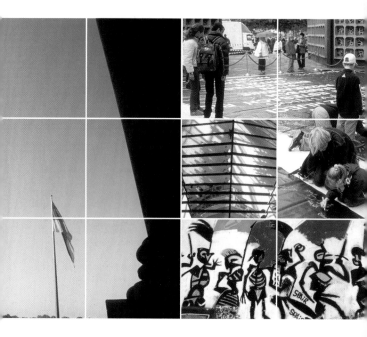

Berlin Now

Visitors inside the glass dome of the Reichstag, designed by Sir Norman Foster

Berlin is shaped by its neighbourhoods, little towns and villages within a city, all with their own unique character and focus. Historically the districts were defined according to class boundaries, but the years of division and the unification that followed have also influenced the character

NEIGHBOURHOODS

• As the name would suggest Mitte is in the middle of the city. Despite being the smallest district it has a great deal to offer and is the undisputed historical, political and cultural heart of the city. The area around Unter den Linden is particularly worth seeing and has some of the best historical buildings in the city. Prenzlauer Berg in the northeast is a young district, but it still has the flair of old Berlin. When the wall came down a mixed crowd of punks, artists and foreigners moved in, transforming the area into a lively and diverse borough. Schöneberg, meaning beautiful hill, is a relaxed and easygoing district in the south attracting successful business types and free thinkers alike. Motzstrasse and Nollendorfplatz are at the heart of the gay day and night scene. Charlottenburg and Wilmersdorff are leafy residential boroughs in the west of the city bordered by the bustling Kurfürstendamm shopping street and the Tiergarten in the east. Kreuzberg in the southeast, the heart of the Turkish community, is famous for its riots, but a decade of stability has transformed it into one of the most diverse and interesting areas of the city with a growing number of good international restaurants and cafés. Off the beaten track, Friedrichshain in the east is also an up-and-coming area popular with students.

Contemporary street sculpture on Mauerstrasse off Friedrichstrasse

of individual areas. There isn't one particular scene in Berlin. There is a niche for everyone; each district has something to offer.

There is little visible evidence of the divide between East and West Berlin. Following the fall of the Wall new businesses and restaurants sprang up everywhere. Growth was rapid and western entrepreneurs moved into former Eastern areas, attracted by tax breaks and development grants. Authentic glimpses of the former east are now only found in museums such as the Haus am Checkpoint Charlie (➤ 42). Change is now part of the fabric of the city and there is a constant turnover of restaurants, clubs and cafés. Luckily things are becoming more sustainable and established in the older districts such as Mitte, Charlottenburg and Prenzlauer Berg.

Berlin is a city of contrast instantly visible in the architecture—old and new, past and present, efficient and relaxed, alternative and conventional, conservative and rebellious. Stark modern buildings sit alongside preserved 18th-century churches, embodying a city accepting its troubled past while moving forward into the future.

A NEW FOCUS

- As well as the eastern and western central city areas, a new heart has emerged between Potsdamer Platz and the government district along the former east/west border. Completely destroyed during World War II, the area was the biggest building site in Europe during the 1990s. Today it is a bustling entertainment and business district, reflecting the progressive and modern architectural face of the city.

11

Above: *Detail of the interior of the Sony Centre in Potsdamer Platz*
Centre: *Strolling along the wide, tree-lined boulevard of Kurfürstendamm*

A CITY OF MUSEUMS

• Berlin is famous for its artistic and historic treasures and has over 170 museums (▶ 52). There is a museum for almost everything–if you can collect it or tell a story about it you will probably find a museum dedicated to it in Berlin.

Controversy continues to rage though about the future of the city. There are still huge areas of the city that remain wastelands, cleared after the bombing of World War II. As money becomes available these areas are being developed, but the debate continues as to how the new city should be shaped, with opinion divided between those who want to preserve old buildings and re-create old areas of the city and those who believe that the time has come to move on both architecturally and psychologically. Investors such as Hugo Boss have campaigned to preserve the old buildings in the city and contributed a great deal of money towards reconstructing some of them around Potsdamer Platz. The expense, however, is huge and they have largely failed to compete with cheaper modern constuction methods and materials and sponsorship from larger corporations such as Daimler Chrysler Benz and Sony. It looks as though the skyline will change inevitably. Some interesting compromises have been made though. Norman Foster's dome in the Reichstag has breathed life and light back into the parliament building, giving access to the public while still preserving its original neo-Renaissance features.

Visitors to Berlin are often surprised by the amount of green space in the heart of the city and the surrounding areas. Nearly a third of Berlin consists of parks meadows, woodland, lakes and rivers. There are more than 16,000ha (39,500 acres) of woodland inside Berlin. Parks, castle grounds, zoos and botanical gardens all

Above: Examining the engravings on the Temple Gate, Ägyptisches Museum

LAKES AND RIVERS

• Berlin is surrounded by lakes, many only a short S-Bahn ride away from the bustling heart of the city. Many visitors dismiss a day trip out of the city because there is so much to see in central Berlin, but excellent transport links make it easy to escape for a day to swim in the cool waters, sunbathe, rent a boat, windsurf and cycle or walk around the lake shore. The most popular is the Grosse Müggelsee to the east of the city. Five rivers run through Berlin— the Spree, the Havel, the Panke, the Wuhle and the Dahme. In addition there is a network of canals criss-crossing the city, the Teltowkanal being the longest. There is even a waterfall in the city, in Viktoria Park in Kreuzberg, a replica of one found in the Polish mountains.

SNACKS

• Snacks are part of the Berlin scene. One of the best known is Currywurst, a large curried sausage. It is hard to visit Berlin without escaping the döner kebab too. Forget kebabs you may have sampled at home, this is the real thing. There are stalls or shops on almost every street corner serving some of the best gourmet Turkish kebabs in the world.

13

Above: *A giant mural at the back of Café Zapata*
Centre: *Tempting confectionary counter in a shop on Friedrichstadt Passage*

provide spaces to relax in and keep the air in the city relatively clean. The Tiergarten, known as 'the green lung', is the biggest park in Berlin. It lies right in the middle of the city, to which it is linked via a network of foot and cycle paths that wind around woods and ponds. Berliners head outside to relax or party in the parks and beer gardens during the summer. The Tiergarten is a popular venue for relaxing, picnics and barbecues and is the site for the Berlin Love Parade in July (▶ 4). The efficient public transport and extensive network of cycle paths are also helping to keep the city green. If you want to get up a little higher for a view over

ART HOTELS

• Art hotels have added a new dimension and provided a much needed lift to the hotel industry in Berlin. Some are more wacky and avant garde that others, but there is a movement to suit every taste. Many are styled floor to ceiling by one artist, while others allow you to choose from a weird and wonderful palette of themed rooms, where even the toilet doubles as a piece of sculpture. Top-class establishements are also responding with a more conventional approach, carefully styling, co-ordinating and lifting the standard of their hotels by employing the services of well-established interior designers or transforming conference spaces and corridors into mini art galleries.

the city, head for the baby hills—Teufelsberg in the west and Müggelberge in the east both 115m (377ft) high.

Berlin is not traditionally thought of as a gastronomic capital, but the quality and range of food available has improved immensely since reunification. The most creative and adventurous restaurants can be found in Mitte and Prenzlauer Berg, but it is easy to find good food all over the city and there is something to suit all tastes. The cuisine reflects the multicultural character of the city and there is a huge variety of restaurants devoted to food from every corner of the globe, to the extent that it is now quite difficult to find one serving traditional German food. Much of the international cuisine has been toned down for the German palate, but there is a growing interest in authentic cooking. You will find everything here from Australian restaurants to Japanese sushi bars. Turkish food is very popular, but some of the best and cheapest food available is Italian. Berliners love pizza and pasta and as a result there is a huge number of Italian restaurants throughout the city competing for business.

Above: High-rise and glass in Potsdamer Platz, the commercial heart of Berlin

FACTS AND FIGURES

- The population of Berlin in 2000 was 3.5 million.
- 46 per cent is male; 54 per cent female. The only Berlin district with more men than women is Kreuzberg.
- 12 per cent of the population is foreign, of which more than one third is Turkish.
- Greater Berlin is the largest city on the European continent.

Berlin Then

Above: *William I, King of Prussia and Emperor of Germany*

THE WALL

In 1961 200,000 people escaped the GDR in the east and fled to the west, 152,000 of them via Berlin. On the night of 12th August 1961 the GDR closed the border, erecting a wall of barbed wire, concrete slabs and stones to halt the flow of refugees. This was followed by the building of the Wall, a 12km (7.5 mile) concrete structure. The border was heavily guarded and during the time the Wall stood 152 people lost their lives trying to escape.

A BERLIN FIRST

Werner Siemens and Johann Georg Malske manufacture the first telegraph in a house on Schöneberger Strasse.

1244 First recorded mention of Berlin.

1369 Berlin becomes a member of the Hanseatic League trading association.

1443 Frederick II of Brandenburg builds the first Berlin castle (Schloss).

1448 Berliners defend their privileges in the 'Berliner Unwille' revolt.

1618– 1648 Berlin is devastated by Austrian and Swedish armies during the Thirty Years' War. The population is halved to less than 6,000.

1701 Elector Frederick III proclaims himself King Frederick I of Prussia. In 1740 Frederick the Great becomes king.

1806 Napoleon enters Berlin.

1848 Germany's 'bourgeois revolution' sees demands for greater middle-class representation in government. Workers take to the barricades.

1871 Berlin becomes capital of a united German Empire under Kaiser Wilhelm I and the Prime Minister of Prussia, Prince Otto von Bismarck.

1918 After World War I, Kaiser Wilhelm II abdicates to make way for a German Republic.

Third left: *Adolf Hitler and the Nazi brass*
Second left: *Berlin's Olympic Stadium, built as part of a massive complex for the ill-fated 1936 Olympics*
Left: *Displays at the Museum Haus am Checkpoint Charlie record escape attempts over the former Berlin Wall*

1920s Despite growing social and economic instability, Berlin becomes a cultural powerhouse. Grosz, Einstein, Brecht and Gropius flourish.

1933 Hitler becomes German Chancellor.

1936 Berlin hosts the Olympic Games.

1938 On the 'night of breaking glass' the Nazis orchestrate the destruction of Jewish properties and synagogues.

1939–45 World War II.

1945 Berlin lies in ruins, its population reduced from 4 million to 2.8 million.

1945–89 A city divided (▶ side panel).

1989 On 9 November the collapse of communism in Eastern Europe leads to the opening of the Berlin Wall and its eventual demise.

1990 Germany is unified.

1999 The first session of the Bundestag in the reopened Reichstag building.

2000 Berlin once again becomes the capital of a united Germany.

2002 Germany adopts the euro.

A CITY DIVIDED

1945 Berlin is divided into four zones of occupation, administered by French, British, US and Soviet forces.
1948–49 A Soviet attempt to force the Western Allies to withdraw from Berlin by blockading the city is foiled by a gigantic airlift of supplies.
1949 Germany is divided into the Federal Republic and the communist German Democratic Republic. Berlin is stranded in the GDR.
1953 Construction workers in East Berlin, protesting at low wages, provoke a full-scale uprising, which is put down by Soviet tanks.
1961 The flood of East Germans to the West is staunched by the building of the Berlin Wall.
1963 John F. Kennedy demonstrates American support for West Berlin in his famous 'Ich bin ein Berliner' speech.

Time to Shop

Berlin is a paradise for shoppers and the city is increasingly trading on its consumer appeal to attract visitors. You can buy everything here from luxury jewellery and designer labels to funky furniture and unusual gifts.

Below: Window of the designer shop Escada on Friedrichstrasse

Above: Shopping meets modern art in the brightly lit arcade of Friedrichstadt Passage

SECOND–HAND

Trend-setters in this style-conscious capital are not afraid to celebrate the past. There are many retro and alternative clothing outlets around Prenzlauer Berg, but if you are serious about second-hand shopping head for the larger outlets such as Colours and Garage (▶ 74) where you buy clothing by the kilo.

Brand shoppers and designer-label fans will be at home among names such as Gucci, Cerruti, Yamamoto and Diesel on Friedrichstrasse. The Kurfürstendamm in the west of the city also has its fair share of the big names, including Versace and Gaultier. There are over a dozen department stores in the city catering to all tastes and trends. The upmarket KaDeWe (Kaufhaus des Westens) just off the Ku'damm, with 43,000sq m (460,000sq ft) of floor space and six floors, is the largest. Galeries Lafayette off Friedrichstrasse has a fantastic food hall in the basement and The Arkaden in Potsdamer Platz has a wide selection of well-known brands on all three floors, with a great selection of restaurants and cafés on the top floor, ideal for refuelling and recharging the batteries after a hard session of retail therapy.

For something a little less mainstream, head for the weird and wonderful shops around Oranienburger Strasse in Mitte, Bergmannstrasse and Oranienstrasse in Kreuzberg and Golzstrasse in Schöneberg for bizarre shoes and bags, crazy clothes and trendy shades and jewellery. Off the beaten track, spend an entertaining afternoon window-shopping or pick up some unique items that you won't find anywhere else in some of the offbeat shops around Kreuzberg and Prenzlauer

Below left: Branch of the designer fashion shop Prada on Kurfürstendamm

Above: Traditional German sausages for a night snack

Berg. Kastanienallee in Prenzlauer Berg is the heart of Berlin's alternative fashion scene and you will find plenty of funky accessories, gifts and quirky up-and-coming designer boutiques and retro Berlin T-shirts and sweatshirts along this trendy street.

There are plenty of shops selling DDR memorabilia and clothing. A daily market in Alexanderplatz sells the genuine articles, such as army uniforms and badges, but shops around Hackescher Markt and Prenzlauer Berg sell retro and cult clothing, accessories and souvenirs paying tribute to the city's history. Look out for souvenirs and clothing bearing the Ampelmann logo, the green-and-red-hat-wearing man seen at stop signs in the former east of the city. Other unique purchases include home-made chocolates found in tempting confectionery shops around the city and fine royal porcelain, both recent and antique items, made by KPM. Also try to seek out a traditional bakery for some of Germany's delicious individual breads.

MARKETS

Berlin has a huge number of flea markets selling clothing, jewellery and antiques. For surprising finds head for the antique market (Wed–Mon) on Georgenstrasse under the S-Bahn bridge. You can pick up some exotic bargains at the Turkish Market on Kollwitzplatz on Thursday afternoons. Weekly street markets are a great place to experience the multicultural tastes of the city. The Winterfeldplatz market on Wednesday and Saturday morning is the best. Mingle among the friendly crowd and sample some Turkish, Italian and Greek delicacies.

19

Out and About

SIGHTSEEING TOURS

**BBS Berliner Bären
Stadtrundfahrt**
Daily tours and days out
in eight languages.
Departures from
Ku'damm and
Alexanderplatz opposite
the Park Inn hotel. ☎ 030
35 19 52 70

**Berolina
Stadtrundfahrten**
Daily bus tours of Berlin
and Potsdam–Sanssouci
in eight languages.
Departures from the
Ku'damm and
Meinekestrasse. ☎ 030
88 56 80 30

Severin and Kühn
Circular city tour and
excursions further afield.
Departures from
Zoologischer Garten
station. ☎ 880 41 90,
www.severin-kuehn-
berlin.de

INFORMATION

WITTENBERG
Distance 58km (36 miles)
Journey Time 1 hour
🚆 From Bahnhof Berlin-
Lichtenberg (trains every
hour)
🏛 Schlossplatz 2
(☎ 03491 49 86 10)
🚢 Boat trips are
available on the River Elb
❓ The town is best
explored on foot

ORGANIZED SIGHTSEEING

For an original view of Berlin, the canal trip offered by the Reederei Heinz Riedel steamboat company (☎ 6 91 37 82) is hard to beat. Departures are from Kottbusser Brücke. For a bit of luxury, you could rent a 14-m (46-ft) yacht with

friends for a cruise on the Havel (Yacht Charter ✉ Berliner Strasse 26–27 ☎ 0331 601 26 88). English-speaking Berliners from Insider Tour give visitors an insider's view of the city during a walk of up to three hours (✉ Boppstrasse 3 ☎ (030 692 3149). The Original Berlin Walks offers two English-language walks: 'Discover Berlin' and 'Infamous Third Reich Sights' (✉ Harbigstrasse 26 ☎ 030 19194).

EXCURSIONS
LUTHERSTADT WITTENBERG

Wittenberg is famous as the cradle of the Reformation. It was here that an obscure monk named Martin Luther began a protest against the Roman Catholic Church that ended in his excommunication and the birth of Protestantism. The Lutherhaus, on Collegien-strasse in the former monastery where Luther later lived, is a vivid museum of the German Reformation. The Castle Church, to which Luther nailed his 95 theses attacking the Church in 1517, is less interesting than the Stadtkirche, which has survived with many of its original features intact, including a beautiful altar panel.

BRANDENBURG

Dominsel, an island in the River Havel, is the charmingly understated focal point of the historic heart of the state of Mark Brandenburg. It was here the first Slav settlers arrived in the 6th century, later founding the Romanesque

cathedral (Dom). This beautiful building survives in its 14th-century Gothic transformation. If this part of the town has a tranquil, almost forgotten air, the Old Town (Altstadt) is more closely attuned to the modern world, although there are historic attractions, notably the market-place with its late Gothic town hall. The New Town (Neustadt) was founded in the late 12th century. There are shops and cafés in its pedestrian zone, but the highlight is the Katherinenkirche, with medieval sculptures and ceiling paintings. The countryside around Brandenburg is outstanding.

LÜBBENAU

Lübbenau is an ideal launching pad for exploring the Spreewald, a scenic wonderland of lakes, canals, farms and inns. The Spreewaldmuseum is near the 19th-century Schloss. The houses around the Marktplatz are worthy examples of the late baroque, as is the Stadtkirche St. Nikolai. An attractive timber-framed building is the only reminder of the old town hall. Also interesting is a Saxon milepost dating from the 18th century. Lübbenau, on the River Spree, is an embarkation point for boat trips and has a small harbour.

INFORMATION

BRANDENBURG
Distance 60km (37 miles)
Journey Time 45 minutes
🚆 From Friedrichstrasse or Zoologischer Garten (trains every hour)
ℹ Haupfstrasse 51 (☎ 03381 22 37 43)
🚢 Boat trips are available on the River Havel
❓ Dominsel is best explored on foot

Far left: *Statue of Martin Luther (Schadow, 1821) in front of the late Gothic (1440) Town Hall in the Markt, Wittenberg*
Left: *Clock tower in historic Brandenburgh*

INFORMATION

LÜBBENAU
Distance 68km (42 miles)
Journey Time 1.5 hours
🚆 From Bahnhof Berlin-Lichtenberg (trains every 2 hours)
ℹ Ernst-von-Houwald-Damm 14 (☎ 03542 30 90)
❓ Best seen from the punting boats that ply the numerous waterways

Walks

THE SIGHTS

- Neue Synagoge
  (➤ 55)
- Monbijou Park
  (➤ 61)
- Sophienkirche
  (➤ 55)
- Elisabethkirche
- Volkspark am
  Weinberg
- Water tower
- Käthe Kollwitz
  memorial

INFORMATION

Distance 5km (3 miles)
Time 2.5 hours
Start point ★
Oranienburger Strasse
🚻 J4
🚇 S-Bahn Oranienburger
Strasse
End point
Husemannstrasse
🚻 K2
🚇 U-Bahn Eberswalder
Strasse
🍴 Café: Café Oren
(➤ 70); Restaurant: Mare
Bê (➤ 67)

PRENZLAUER BERG AND THE SCHEUNENVIERTEL

Walk eastward along Oranienburger Strasse, heart of the Scheunenviertel (Barn Quarter), which became the Jewish Quarter in the late 17th century. Dominating the skyline is the golden dome of the Neue Synagoge (New Synagogue). Lower down, on the right, is Monbijou Park, once the grounds of a royal palace, and, on the left, the remains of the Old Jewish Cemetery, destroyed by the Nazis.

Turn left into Rosenthaler Strasse and then take the first left into Sophienstrasse. This neighbourhood is now an artists' enclave. Between Sophienstrasse and Oranienburger Strasse are the historic courtyards known as the Hackesche Höfe. These 19th-century workers' houses and factory workshops are now smart restaurants, boutiques, art galleries and theatres.

Continue along Sophienstrasse, passing the 18th-century Sophienkirche, then follow Grosse Hamburger Strasse. No. 11, 'The Missing House,' commemorates its occupants, who were all killed in an Allied bombing raid. Cross Kopperplatz into Ackerstrasse, the heart of an old working-class quarter.

On the opposite side of Invalidenstrasse are the remains of Schinkel's Elisabethkirche (1832). Walk east along Veteranenstrasse, past the Volkspark am Weinberg and join Kastanienallee briefly before turning right into Schwedter Strasse. Cross Senefelderplatz into Kollwitzstrasse. On the right, just off Belforter Strasse, is the 19th-century water tower used by the Nazis as a makeshift torture chamber in 1933. At Kollwitzplatz is a memorial to the Expressionist artist Käthe Kollwitz.

Husemannstrasse now has a lively café scene, but the refurbished tenements disguise a more squalid late 19th-century working-class life.

The gilded dome of the restored Moorish-style Synagogue on Berlin's Oranienburger Strasse

Schöneberg

Admire the art-deco interior of Wittenbergplatz station, then walk down Kleiststrasse to Nollendorfplatz, the centre of 1920s nightlife, and still home to the Metropol, dating from 1906 (formerly a theatre, now a nightclub). Walk south along Maassenstrasse, crossing Nollendorfstrasse. British author Christopher Isherwood, whose reminiscences of Berlin life in the 1930s inspired the film *Cabaret*, lived at Nollendorfstrasse 17. The next square you come to, Winterfeldtplatz, has a twice-weekly market.

At the end of Maassenstrasse is Pallasstrasse; the Sportspalast that once stood here was the scene of many of Hitler's rallies. The flak tower nearby was a wartime survivor and was part of the city's defences. Cross Pallasstrasse into Elssholzstrasse. On the left is Kleistpark, named after the Romantic poet Heinrich von Kleist, who shot himself on the shores of the Wannsee in 1811, aged only 34. Just inside the park is the former Supreme Court of Justice (Kammergericht), where Count von Stauffenberg and other instigators of the failed July Bomb Plot to assassinate Hitler were tried in 1944. A few months later the judge, the infamous Roland Freisler, was killed when the building sustained a direct hit during an Allied bombing raid.

Turn right into Grunewaldstrasse, then left into Martin-Luther-Strasse. Dominating John-F-Kennedy-Platz is the Rathaus Schöneberg, former town hall of West Berlin. It was from the balcony of this building that President Kennedy delivered his famous 'Ich bin ein Berliner' speech.

THE SIGHTS

- U-Bahn Wittenbergplatz (➤ 62)
- The Metropol
- Nollendorfstrasse 17
- Winterfeldtmarkt (➤ 77)
- Kleistpark
- Rathaus Schöneberg

INFORMATION

Distance 5km (3 miles)
Time 2.5 hours
Start ★ U-Bahn Wittenbergplatz
🚇 F7
Ⓤ U-Bahn Wittenbergplatz
End point Rathaus Schöneberg
🚇 F9
Ⓤ U-Bahn Rathaus Schöneberg
🍴 Café: Tim's Canadian Deli (➤ 71)
❓ First mentioned in 1264 as Sconenberch, the residential quarter of Berlin now known as Schöneberg was not formally incorporated into the city until 1920.

Banks of fresh fruit and vegetables in the open-air Winterfeldtplatz Market

Berlin by Night

Above: *The Brandenburger Tor or Brandenburg Gate illuminated at night*
Above right: *View of Potsdamer Platz, with the Daimler Benz building on the right*

LISTINGS

Useful listings magazines include *Prinz*, *Tip*, *Zitty* (all twice-monthly, in German); *Berlin TutGut* (from Tourist Information, in English); *Berlin Das Magazin* (quarterly, in English and German); *Berlin Programm* (monthly, in German). *Prinz* also publishes an annual magazine picking out the best restaurants, shops, bars, clubs and hotels in the city. Berlin Tourismus Marketing publishes *Berlin-Kalendar* every two months in English and German.

24-HOUR PARTY

Nightlife continues well into the morning in Berlin as there are no licensing hours restricting opening time. Many bars and pubs are quiet before 10pm and things don't really get going until after midnight. The latest place to meet before the party starts though is the after-work club, catering to early evening revellers, and there is a growing number of lounges opening up encouraging you to wind down and relax before you hit the town.

CLUBS

Berlin's club scene is split into two categories: institutions that have stood the test of time and single occasion parties playing the latest sounds publicized via word of mouth within the extremely prolific undergound scene. It can be tricky to penetrate this on a short visit, but it is worth tracking down one of the best clubs in Berlin, the legendary WMF club, which moves to different venues on a regular basis. Established clubs are probably the best bet, but you should check out the latest listings as most have very diverse programmes and certain nights may not be to your taste. There is plenty to choose from though, from salsa and techno to electro punk and drum 'n' bass.

PERFORMANCE

The cultural scene in Berlin is buzzing. From traditional opera houses and cabarets to experimental theatre, live jazz and new metal bands, the city's entertainment and live events programme caters to all tastes.

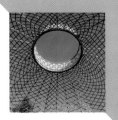

BERLIN's
top 25 sights

The sights are shown on the maps on the inside front cover and inside back cover, numbered **1**–**25** from west to east across the city

1 Sanssouci *26*

2 Cecilienhof *27*

3 Klein-Glienicke *28*

4 Spandau Zitadelle *29*

5 Jagdschloss Grunewald *30*

6 Sachsenhausen *31*

7 Ethnologisches Museum *32*

8 Schloss Charlottenburg *33*

9 Kurfürstendamm *34*

10 Kaiser-Wilhelm-Gedächtniskirche *35*

11 Bauhaus-Archiv *36*

12 Kulturforum *37*

13 Kunstgewerbemuseum *38*

14 Tiergarten *39*

15 Potsdamer Platz *40*

16 Brandenburger Tor *41*

17 Checkpoint Charlie *42*

18 Gendarmenmarkt *43*

19 Unter den Linden *44*

20 Museumsinsel *45*

21 Pergamon Museum *46*

22 Berliner Dom *47*

23 Nikolaiviertel *48*

24 Alexanderplatz *49*

25 Schloss Köpenick *50*

Sanssouci

HIGHLIGHTS

- Schloss Sanssouci
- Terraces and Great Fountain
- Grave of Frederick the Great
- Neptune grotto
- Orangery
- Friedenskirche
- Sicilian gardens
- Roman Baths (Römische Bäder)
- New Palace (Neues Palais)
- Ape bearing Voltaire's features, on the Chinese Teahouse

INFORMATION

www.spsg.de

➕ Off map to southwest; Locator map off C4

✉ Maulbeerallee, Potsdam

☎ 0331 969 42 02

🕐 Schloss Sanssouci: Apr–end Oct Tue–Sun 9–5; Nov–end Mar Tue–Sun 9–4
New Palace: Apr–end Oct Tue–Sun 9–12.30, 1–5; Nov–end Mar Tue–Sun 9–12.30, 1–4

🍴 Café; restaurant

🚇 S-Bahn Potsdam-Stadt

🚌 Bus 695; tram 96, 98

🅿 Wild Park

♿ Few

🎟 Park: free
Schloss: expensive (guided tour only)
New Palace: moderate

🔗 Cecilienhof (▶ 27)

Frederick the Great's celebrated Sanssouci was a place of relaxation and peaceful seclusion where the Prussian monarch could get away from it all. The eccentric Chinese Teahouse epitomizes his ideal.

Two palaces On the western edge of Potsdam, just 19km (12 miles) from Berlin (about 30 minutes by train or car), you'll find landscaped Sanssouci Park. It contains two quite different yet equally impressive palaces built for Frederick the Great. Formal gardens, terraces, fountains and follies complete the picture. Don't be put off by the crowds around Schloss Sanssouci. Other sights and the grounds are much less congested.

Schloss Sanssouci Frederick's celebrated retreat was designed by a friend, Georg Wenzeslaus von Knobelsdorff. The single-storey rococo façade, topped by a shallow green dome, conceals a succession of gorgeously furnished rooms and a collection of precious objects including sculptures, painted vases and elaborate clocks. The French philosopher Voltaire was Sanssouci's most famous guest—eventually he fell out with Frederick, who said disparagingly 'he has the slyness and will of an ape'.

New Palace If Sanssouci is the perfect reflection of Frederick the Great's cultivated side, then the New Palace (Neues Palais) reveals his obsession with self-aggrandisement. The best view of the expansive red-brick façade is from the imposing driveway, intended both to intimidate and impress courtiers and foreign visitors. Johann Büring designed the façade, and Karl von Gontard the sumptuous interior. About a dozen of the palace's more than 200 rooms are open to the public.

Cecilienhof

A trip to Potsdam Town, rewarding in itself, can easily be combined with an excursion to this unusual palace, which, in July 1945, hosted the Potsdam Conference while Berlin and its environs lay in ruins.

Potsdam Conference Set just north of Potsdam in an area of parkland called the Neuer Garten, Schloss Cecilienhof was the setting for the last great inter-Allied government conference of World War II, ostensibly convened to redraw the post-war map of Europe. The leading delegates were the so-called 'Big Three': Winston Churchill, representing Great Britain; Harry S. Truman of the United States; and, heading the Soviet delegation, Josef Stalin. You can see the conference hall and the studies and reception rooms of the various delegations.

Semi-rural retreat Schloss Cecilienhof, completed in 1917, was commissioned by Kaiser Wilhelm II for his son Wilhelm. Ironically this semi-rural retreat, constructed during World War I, was built in the style of an English country house. The Hohenzollerns occupied the palace until 1945.

Grounds Much older than the palace itself are the buildings on the grounds, notably the Marmorpalais, conceived by Karl von Gontard in 1787–89. Grapevines grew here in abundance—there were more than 40 vineyards in the 18th century. The Dutch-style servants' quarters mirror the style of the celebrated Dutch Quarter in Potsdam Town. Also of interest are the original garden houses, orangery and ruined library.

HIGHLIGHTS

- Conference table
- Offices of the three powers
- Tudor-style chimneys
- Marmorpalais
- Ruined library
- Shingle House
- Carved oak staircase
- Sphinx on the Orangery

INFORMATION

www.spsg.de
- Off map to southwest; Locator map off C4
- Neuer Garten
- 0331 969 42 44
- Apr–end Oct Tue–Sun 10–5; Nov–end Mar Sat, Sun 10–4
- Restaurant
- S-Bahn Potsdam-Stadt
- Bus 694; tram 92
- Potsdam-Stadt
- None
- Moderate

Cecilienhof's 'Tudor' chimneys

Klein-Glienicke

The park surrounding this elegant villa and former royal residence is perched decoratively on the banks of the Jungfernsee, between Berlin and Potsdam. Just outside the park gate is the Glienicker Bridge, famous as a setting for Cold War spy novels.

The Schloss and park The mock-Renaissance Schloss was designed in 1824 by Karl Friedrich Schinkel for Prince Friedrich Karl of Prussia, the brother of Kaiser Wilhelm I. Nowadays the grounds are known for their arcadian follies and ornamental garden. The follies are by Schinkel, and the park was laid out by Peter Lenné, also responsible for the Berlin Tiergarten. Looking for rhyme or reason in the choice of follies is a fruitless exercise, although the themes of Renaissance Italy and Classical Greece can be detected here and there. The most extraordinary flight of fancy must be the Klosterhof. These remains are genuinely Italian: the cloister came from a monastery near Venice, while the capital decorated with the chained monkey once belonged to Pisa's famous Leaning Tower.

Glienicker Brücke Just outside the gate is the Glienicker Bridge, which spans the Havel at the southern end of the Jungfernsee to link Berlin with Potsdam. Unremarkable in itself, the bridge came to the world's attention in 1962 when, marking the border between East and West, it was the scene of a swap involving the US pilot Gary Powers, who had been shot down by the Soviet air force on allegations of spying in the famous U-2 incident. The bridge subsequently starred in films and spy novels and became a symbol of the Cold War.

HIGHLIGHTS

- Ornamental gardens
- Lion fountain
- Casino with pergolas
- Relics from the Temple of Poseidon
- Rotunda (Grosse Neugierde)
- Teahouse (Kleine Neugierde)
- Stibadium, pavilion
- Klosterhof
- Glienicker Bridge (Glienicker Brücke)
- View of Havel

INFORMATION

www.spsg.de

- Off map to southwest; Locator map off C4
- ✉ Königstrasse 36
- ☎ 0331 969 42 02
- Park: daily 7am–8pm
  Schloss: 15 May–15 Oct
  Sat, Sun 10–5
- 🍴 Excellent restaurant
- Ⓢ S-Bahn Wannsee
- 🚌 Bus 116
- Potsdam-Stadt
- ♿ None
- Inexpensive
- ↔ Cecilienhof (▶ 27)

Spandau Zitadelle

Of the many attractive villages on Berlin's outskirts, a favourite is ancient Spandau with its red-brick Zitadelle, picturesque streets and views across the Havel. The best vantage point is the Juliusturm, the oldest surviving part of the Zitadelle.

The Zitadelle A strategic location at the confluence of the rivers Spree and Havel made Spandau important in the Middle Ages. The first Zitadelle (fortress), dating from the 12th century, was rebuilt by Joachim III in 1557. The oldest surviving part of the building is the crenellated Juliusturm—the view from the top of the tower is worth the steep climb. Most of the bastions and outbuildings date from the 19th-century, though not the Old Magazine, which is as ancient as the castle itself.

Many lives Spandau castle briefly housed a laboratory for developing incendiary rockets in the early 19th century. Now part of it is a museum. One exhibit is an 1860 cannon, brought back from Siberia, where it had languished for more than a century. The fortress last saw active service during the Napoleonic Wars, when the Old Arsenal was reduced to ruins. Just inside the castle gateway is the statue of a defiant Albrecht, the famous Bear of Brandenburg.

Altstadt Spandau The attractive Old Town is only a short walk from the castle. The Gothic house (Gotisches Haus) in Breite Strasse dates from 1232, and in the central square, Reformationsplatz, are cafés and the Nikolaikirche. North of here lies the quaint old area known as the Kolk, and close by is Spandau's busy lock on the Havel.

HIGHLIGHTS

- Cannons
- Statue of Albrecht the Bear
- Museum of the Middle Ages
- Juliusturm
- Bastion walls
- Old Magazine
- Ruined arsenal
- Kolk and Spandau lock

INFORMATION

- ⊞ Off map to west; Locator map A4
- ✉ Strasse Am Juliusturm
- ☎ 030 35 494 42 00
- 🕐 Tue–Fri 9–5, Sat, Sun 10–5
- 🍴 Am Juliusturm (Zitadelle, ► 62)
- Ⓤ U-Bahn Zitadelle
- 🚌 Bus 133
- 🚉 Spandau
- ♿ Few 💶 Inexpensive

Detail on the Zitadelle

Jagdschloss Grunewald

HIGHLIGHTS

Jagdschloss Grunewald
- Hunting museum
- *Adam and Eve and Judith*, Lucas Cranach the Elder
- *Susannah and the Elders*, Jacob Jordaens
- *Julius Caesar*, Rubens
- Wooden ceiling in Great Hall
- Trompe-l'oeil stonework

Grunewald Forest
- Grunewaldsee
- Grunewaldturm

INFORMATION

Jagdschloss Grunewald
- ✚ Off map to west; Locator map B3
- ✉ Am Grunewaldsee, near Hüttenweg
- ☎ 030 81 33 35 97
- 🕑 Mid-May–mid-Oct Tue–Sun 10–5; mid-Oct–mid-May Sat, Sun 10–4
- 🚌 Bus 115, 183
- ♿ None 💷 Inexpensive
- ↔ Brücke Museum (▶ 54)

Grunewaldturm
- ✚ Off map to west; Locator map B3
- ✉ Havelchaussee 61
- ☎ 03 03 04 12 03
- 🕑 Tower: daily 10am–dusk (10–midnight in summer)
- 🍴 Café 🕑 Mon–Fri 11–11; Sat, Sun 9.30am–11pm
- 🚌 Bus 218 ♿ None
- 💷 Inexpensive

The Grunewald forest is an amazing woodland on the western edge of Berlin. The dreamily scenic 32sq km (12sq miles), dotted with lakes, beaches and nature reserves, are a favourite playground of Berliners at weekends.

Hunting lodge Jagdschloss Grunewald is an attractive Renaissance hunting lodge, built in 1542 for Elector Joachim II of Brandenburg. The stables and outbuildings date from around 1700, when the house was surrounded by a moat. Today the lodge is a museum decorated with paintings and furniture from various royal collections; the chase is the predominant theme. One picture shows Kaiser Wilhelm on a visit to the Grunewald. The 17th-century Dutch school is well represented among the paintings on display, but the best work is by a German, Lucas Cranach the Elder, who has an entire room to himself. Equally remarkable is the painted wooden ceiling of the Great Hall (Grosser Saal) on the ground floor. This is the only surviving 16th-century room. Across the courtyard, the barn has been converted into a hunting museum.

Grunewald Forest Native trees, felled for fuel after the war, have been replanted. Paths criss-cross the forest, beaches fringe the Havel and there is space for leisure pursuits from boating to hang-gliding. You can swim in the Grunewaldsee, site of the hunting lodge, and in the Krumme Lanke. Between these two lakes is a marshy nature reserve known as the Langes Luch. For views, climb the Grunewaldturm, a 72m (236ft) folly on the banks of the Havel, built for Kaiser Wilhelm II in 1897. A second vantage point is the Teufelsberg (Devil's Mountain), an artificial hill made from wartime rubble.

Sachsenhausen

Some 100,000 prisoners perished at this concentration camp during World War II. The great lie 'Work makes you free', inscribed on the entrance gate, is a chilling reminder of the deception and evil once practised here.

Nerve centre The Nazis opened the camp in July 1936, just as Berlin was preparing to host the Olympic Games. Sachsenhausen was the headquarters of the concentration camp inspectorate, and there was a training school here.

Museums The two museums tell the terrible story of the camp. One focuses on the plight of the Jews; the other, in the former kitchens, displays various artefacts and other illustrations of daily life. Some of the cells in the cell block have been restored in memory of the heroes of the German and international resistance to Fascism. Outside are three wooden execution posts.

Sachsenhausen today

Extermination camp Two of the original prison huts have been preserved, as well as the perimeter walls, parade ground, fences and watchtowers. 'Station Z', where prisoners were murdered—some were shot, some were gassed—before their bodies were cremated, occupies one corner of the site. The furnishings and tiled walls of the pathology department have been preserved. Here corpses were dissected for experimental purposes. Films on various aspects of camp history are shown in the what was the former laundry.

INFORMATION

✚ Off map to northwest; Locator map off A3
✉ Strasse der Nationen 22
☎ 03301 20 00
🕐 Mar–end Oct Tue–Sun 8.30–6; Oct–end Mar 8.30–4
🍴 None
🚇 S-Bahn Oranienburg (then 20-minute walk)
🚌 Oranienburg
♿ Few
💷 Free

Ethnologisches Museum

HIGHLIGHTS

- Polynesian clubhouse
- Oceanian boats
- Pre-Columbian gold statuettes
- Peruvian pottery
- Throne and footstool from Cameroon
- Benin bronzes
- Indonesian shadow puppets
- Sri Lankan carved masks
- Australian bark painting
- World music headphones

INFORMATION

www.smpk.de

- Off map to south; Locator map B3
- Lansstrasse 8
- 030 20 90 55 55 (info)
- Tue–Fri 10–6, Sat–Sun 11–6
- Café
- U-Bahn Dahlem-Dorf
- Bus 110, 183, X11
- Lichterfelde West
- Good
- Inexpensive
- Botanischer Garten (➤ 58)

The folk art theme extends beyond the Ethnological Museum to the nearby Dahlem-Dorf U-Bahn station, where modern primitivist sculptures offer provocative seating. Test them for comfort, then make your own artistic judgment.

Exhibitions Although the airy rooms of the Ethnologisches Museum appear large, there is exhibition space for only a fraction of its 400,000-plus ethnological items. Only Oceania and the Americas are represented by permanent exhibitions. Africa, East Asia and South Asia are covered in temporary displays.

Oceania The Oceanian boats are probably the highlight of the collection. The display includes an 18th-century vessel known as a Tongiaki from Tonga, which resembles a catamaran. For landlubbers there is the fantastically decorated male clubhouse, from the Palau Islands of the western Pacific.

Pre-Columbian art The focus of the American collection is the exhibition of ancient sculptures and figurines, mainly from México and Peru.

Gold was the medium favoured by many of these artists and the craftsmanship represented here is perhaps among the best of its kind in the world. Just as beautiful, and more arresting, are the decorated stone *steles* from Cozumalhuapa (Guatemala), created to fend off evil spirits.

Schloss Charlottenburg

This attractive former royal palace, built in the rococo style, lies in its own grounds only a stone's throw from the heart of Berlin. The highlights of the Schloss itself have to be the gorgeous White Hall and Golden Gallery, in the New Wing.

Royal retreat The Schloss was built over more than 100 years, and its development mirrors the aggrandisement of the Prussian dynasty of Hohenzollern, recalled in the forecourt by Andreas Schlüter's superb equestrian statue of the Great Elector, which once stood outside the Berlin Schloss. The Electress Sophie Charlotte's rural retreat—this suburb of Berlin was still deep in the countryside and considered suitable for a summer palace—designed by Arnold Nering in 1695, was transformed into the palace you see today during the reigns of Frederick I and Frederick II by the architect Georg Wenzeslaus von Knobelsdorff. The Great Orangery and Theatre form wings of the Palace, as does the Langhans Building, now the Museum of Pre- and Early History.

Riverside grounds Do not leave Schloss Charlottenburg without seeing the delightful grounds, which slope toward the River Spree. The formal French garden is a marked contrast to the landscaped English garden, which houses the Mausoleum built for Queen Luise, and the Belvedere, now a museum devoted to Berlin porcelain. Closer to the palace, do not miss the delightfully idiosyncratic Neue Pavilion, designed by Berlin's best-known 19th-century architect, Karl Friedrich Schinkel.

HIGHLIGHTS

- White Hall
- Golden Gallery
- Gobelins' rooms
- Study and bedchamber of Frederick I
- *Embarkation for Cythera*, J-A Watteau (above)
- Statue of the Great Elector
- Schinkel Pavilion
- Great Orangery
- Gardens

A familiar landmark

INFORMATION

- ✚ B5; Locator map D4
- ✉ Charlottenburg, Luisenplatz
- ☎ 0331 969 42 02
- 🕐 Alte Schloss: Tue–Fri 9–5, Sat, Sun 10–5. Neue Flügel: Tue–Fri 10–6, Sat, Sun 11–6
- 🍴 Restaurant
- Ⓤ U-Bahn Richard-Wagner-Platz, Sophie-Charlotte-Platz
- 🚌 Bus 109, 210, X21, 145
- ♿ Few 🅿 Moderate   33

Kurfürstendamm

HIGHLIGHTS

- Literaturhaus
- Käthe-Kollwitz-Museum
- Fasanenstrasse
- Iduna House
- Hotel Kempinski Bristol
  (➤ 86)
- Neoclassical news-stands

INFORMATION

www.kaethe-kollwitz.de

➕ E7; Locator map F4

🚇 U-Bahn Kurfürstendamm;
U-Bahn Uhlandstrasse;
S-Bahn Zoologischer
Garten

🚌 Bus 109, 119, 129, 219

🚉 Zoologischer Garten

🔄 Kaiser-Wilhelm-
Gedächtniskirche (➤ 35)

**Literaturhaus and
Wintergarten Café**

✉ Fasanenstrasse 23

☎ 030 882 50 44

🕐 Mon–Fri 10–8, Sat 10–4

🍴 Excellent

♿ Few

🎫 Free

Käthe-Kollwitz-Museum

✉ Fasanenstrasse 24

☎ 030 882 52 10

🕐 Wed–Mon 11–6

♿ Few

🎫 Moderate

It would be unthinkable to come to Berlin without visiting the Ku'damm, which stretches for 3km (2 miles) towards Charlottenburg. The city's celebrated tree-lined boulevard is usually buzzing with pavement cafés, restaurants and Berlin's major shops.

Shopping street Many of the Ku'damm stores were the beneficiaries of the *Wirtschaftswunder*, the economic miracle of the 1960s, which was brought about partly by American investment.

New West End The elegant streets off the Ku'damm—Fasanenstrasse, for example—were a part of the New West End, which was developed as a residential area at the end of the 19th century. Many of the houses here are now art galleries; an exception is the museum devoted to the life and work of the 20th-century artist Käthe Kollwitz at Fasanenstrasse 24. Next door to the museum is the Literaturhaus, a cultural centre with a secluded garden café, the Wintergarten. The Villa Grisebach at No. 25 is an outstanding example of Jugendstil architecture. A little further away, on the corner of Leibnizstrasse, is another period piece, the Iduna House, whose unmistakable cupola dates from 1907.

Coffee shops Despite rising rents on the Ku'damm, the café tradition in Berlin still lives on in the old name of Kranzler. Johann Georg Kranzler opened the first coffee shop in Berlin in 1835, on the corner of Friedrichstrasse. These days, tourists and literati have taken the place of the Prussian aristocracy who once frequented the many cafés; join them for a while to rest your legs, enjoy a superb coffee and watch the world go by.

Kaiser-Wilhelm-Gedächtniskirche

The blackened ruin of this church— bombed in 1943, now a reminder of the futility of war—casts its shadow over the Ku'damm. Particularly moving is the cross of nails given by the people of Coventry in England, another war-torn city.

War memorial The Gedächtniskirche was Kaiser Wilhelm II's contribution to the developing New West End. Built in 1895 in Romanesque style, it was always rather incongruous in this proudly modern section of the city. No expense was spared on the interior, and the dazzling mosaics are deliberately reminiscent of St. Mark's in Venice. After Allied bombs destroyed the church in 1943, the shell was allowed to stand. Poignant in its way, the old building now serves as a small museum focusing on the wartime destruction.

The New Chapel Berliners have denigrated the octagonal chapel and hexagonal stained-glass tower, both uncompromisingly modern (the 'make-up box' and the 'lipstick tube' are favoured nicknames). However, many visitors find peace in the blue-hued chapel, whose stained glass is from Chartres, France. The chapel was designed by Egon Eiermann in the early 1960s.

Breitscheidplatz In shameless contrast, brash Breitscheidplatz proclaims the values of a materialistic culture, only partially redeemed by the colourful street musicians and occasional fund-raising stunts. Nowadays it is a refuge for Berlin's down-and-outs and is routinely targeted by the police. The focus is the Globe Fountain (Weltkugelbrunnen).

HIGHLIGHTS

- Cross of nails
- Surviving mosaics
- The Stalingrad Madonna
- Bell tower
- Globe Fountain

INFORMATION

www.gedaechtniskirche.com

- E6; Locator map E3
- Breitscheidplatz
- 030 218 50 23
- Memorial Hall: Mon–Sat 10–4. New Chapel: daily 9–7
- U- or S-Bahn Zoologischer Garten, U-Bahn Kurfürstendamm
- Bus 100, 109, 119, 129, 146
- Zoologischer Garten
- Few
- Free

Breitscheidplatz

Bauhaus-Archiv

HIGHLIGHTS

- Walter Gropius's building
- Marcel Breuer's leather armchair
- Metal-framed furniture
- Ceramics
- Moholy-Nagy's sculpture *Light-space-modulator*
- Designs and models of Bauhaus buildings
- Paintings by Paul Klee
- Paintings by Vassily Kandinsky
- Schlemmer's theatre designs
- Marianne Brandt's tea and coffee set

INFORMATION

www.bauhaus.de
- F6; Locator map E3
- Klingelhöferstrasse 14
- 030 254 00 20
- Wed–Mon 10–5
- Café
- U-Bahn Nollendorfplatz
- Bus 100, 129, 187, 341
- Bellevue
- Good
- Moderate
- Kulturforum (➤ 37), Tiergarten (➤ 39)

Brush up on your knowledge of the history of design by visiting one of Berlin's foremost cultural totems—a museum celebrating the Bauhaus, one of the most influential art and design movements of the 20th century.

End of decoration In the traumatic aftermath of World War I all values, artistic ones included, came under scrutiny. In Germany, the dynamic outcome was the Bauhaus school, founded in 1919 by Walter Gropius in Weimar, the capital of the recently founded Republic. Gropius and his disciples stressed function, rather than decoration, favouring modern materials such as concrete and tubular steel for their versatility and appearance.

Interdisciplinary approach Mass production guaranteed the Bauhaus an unprecedented influence on European and transatlantic architecture and design. Most remarkable, perhaps, was the school's insistence on collaboration between different artistic disciplines. Workshops in metalwork, print and advertising, photography, painting and ceramics were coordinated by a cohort of outstanding team leaders, among them Vassily Kandinsky, Paul Klee, Oskar Schlemmer and Laszlo Moholy-Nagy.

Legacy The revolutionary credentials of the Bauhaus drove it into conflict with the Nazis. Already forced to move to Dessau and then to Berlin, the school closed in 1933 but its influence lives on in the design of furniture and appliances found in many homes today.

Exhibition The display, ranging from furniture to sketches, is housed in a small museum designed by Walter Gropius in 1964.

Kulturforum

Conceived in the 1960s by Hans Scharoun, the Kulturforum complex is controversial as architecture. But no one can dispute the beauty of the collections in the Gemäldegalerie and the Neue Nationalgalerie.

Gemäldegalerie The picture gallery, an outstanding collection, comprises more than 1,450 paintings of the 13th to 18th centuries. Dürer, Hans Holbein, Lucas Cranach the Elder and other German masters are well represented, as are the great Dutch artists Van Eyck, Rogier van der Weyden and Pieter Bruegel. Dutch baroque painting is also prominent, with several outstanding works by Rembrandt, among others. The Italian collection reads like a roll-call of great Renaissance artists: Fra Angelico, Piero della Francesco, Giovanni Bellini and Raphael. Outside, in the sculpture park, you can see works by Henry Moore and others.

Neue Nationalgalerie Designed by Bauhaus architect Mies van der Rohe for the hanging of large canvases, the New National Gallery concentrates on international modern art. Many leading post-war artists are represented here: Robert Rauschenberg, Roy Lichtenstein, Frank Stella, Joseph Beuys. The lower floor displays work by 20th-century Europeans, including Kirchner, Magritte, Klee, Max Ernst, Otto Dix, de Chirico, Dalí and Picasso.

Musikinstrumenten-Museum In the Museum of Musical Instruments you'll see almost everything from bagpipes to synthesizers. The world's first bass tuba is here, and don't miss the Orchestron organ. The policy is no-touch, but you can listen to tapes of the instruments in performance on strategically placed headphones.

HIGHLIGHTS

Gemäldegalerie
- *Netherlandish Proverbs*, Bruegel
- *Portrait of Enthroned Madonna and Child*, Botticelli
- *Portrait of Georg Gisze*, Rembrandt

Neue Nationalgalerie
- *Pillars of Society*, Grosz
- *Departure of the Ships*, Klee
- *L'Idée Fixe*, Magritte

INFORMATION

- www.smpk.de
- G6; Locator map E2
- Matthäikircheplatz 8
- Gemäldegalerie and Neue Nationalgalerie: 030 20 90 55 55. Musikinstrumenten-Museum: 030 25 48 11 78
- Gemäldegalerie: Tue–Thu 10–10, Sun 10–6. Neue Nationalgalerie: Tue–Fri 10–6, Thu 10–10, Sat–Sun 11–6. Musikinstrumenten-Museum: Tue–Fri 9–5, Sat–Sun 10–5
- Cafés
- U- or S-Bahn Potsdamer Platz
- Bus 129, 148, 200, 248, 341, 348
- Good
- Moderate; additional charge for temporary exhibitions in the Neue Nationalgalerie

37

Kunstgewerbemuseum

HIGHLIGHTS

- 8th-century Burse reliquary
- Frederick Barbarossa's baptismal bowl
- J. J. Kaendler's Harlequin Group
- Lidded goblet of gold ruby glass from Potsdam
- Lüneburg silver
- Gold elephant fountain from Köln
- Guelph reliquary from Köln
- Majolica love dish from Urbino
- Art-deco stained-glass windows
- 'Wiggle-chair' by Frank Gehry

INFORMATION

www.smpk.de
- G6; Locator map E2
- Matthäikirchplatz
- 030 20 90 55 55
- Tue–Fri 10–6; Sat–Sun 11–6
- Café
- U- or S-Bahn Potsdamer Platz
- Bus 129, 142, 148, 248, 348
- Good
- Inexpensive
- Bauhaus-Archiv (➤ 36), Kulturforum (➤ 37), Tiergarten (➤ 39)

Berlin's wonderful collection of arts and crafts is in the Museum of Applied Art in the Kulturforum. Look for the 8th-century Burse reliquary of Enger, an enamelled wooden box inlaid with gold and studded with silver, pearls and precious gems.

Cultural riches The vast collections are arranged chronologically on several floors. Every conceivable kind of applied art is displayed, including gold and silver work, glassware, majolica, jewellery, porcelain, furniture and clothing. A counterpoint to the medieval treasures assembled from churches and abbeys all over Germany is the Lüneburg Town Hall silver, evidence of the great wealth acquired by the burghers of the Hanseatic town in the 15th and 16th centuries.

Kunstkammer The museum's collection is based on the 7,000 objects acquired by the Brandenburg Kunstkammer (Cabinet of Curiosities) from the 17th century onwards. An intriguing item is the Pommersche Kunstschrank, a wonderfully eclectic assortment of objects from surgical instruments to hairbrushes and miniature books. It was assembled between 1610 and 1616 for the Duke of Pommern-Stettin.

Porcelain and art deco Painted figurines from Meissen are the highlight of the porcelain collection. The Jugendstil glass, ceramics and jewellery are gorgeous—look for the intricate ornamental fastener made by Lalique in around 1900. On the ground floor is a display of art-deco furniture.

Porcelain figure dated 1780

Tiergarten

Boating, strolling, jogging, summer concerts, ornamental gardens—this huge park 202ha (550 acres) in the centre of Berlin offers all this and more. Look for the antique gas lamps from various European cities along the route from the station to the Landwehrkanal.

Hunting ground *Tiergarten* means 'animal garden', recalling a time when the park was stocked with wild boar and deer for the pleasure of the Prussian aristocracy. It was landscaped by Peter Joseph Lenné in the 1830s and still bears his imprint—remarkably, since the park was almost totally destroyed in World War II.

Siegessäule The Siegessäule (victory column) occupies a prime site on Strasse des 17 Juni, although it originally stood in front of the Reichstag. Erected in 1873 to commemorate Prussian victories against Denmark, Austria and France, the 67m (220ft) column is decorated with captured cannon. 'Gold Else', the victory goddess on the summit, beloved by Berliners, is waving her laurel wreath wryly towards Paris.

War heroes and revolutionaries The three heroes of the Wars of Unification—Count Otto von Bismarck and Generals Helmut von Moltke and Albrecht von Roon—are fêted with statues to the north of the Siegessäule. Memorials to two prominent revolutionaries, Karl Liebknecht and Rosa Luxemburg, stand beside the Landwehrkanal near Lichtensteinallee. Their bodies were dumped in the canal in 1919 by members of the right-wing Free Corps who had shot them shortly after an abortive Communist uprising.

HIGHLIGHTS

- Zoologischer Garten (► 61)
- Kongresshalle
- Carillon
- Bismarck monument
- Schloss Bellevue
- Neuer See
- English Garden
- Soviet War Memorial

INFORMATION

Siegessäule

- ✚ F5; Locator map E2
- ✉ Grossen Stern, Strasse des 17 Juni
- ☎ 030 391 29 61
- 🕐 Mon–Thu 9.30–6.30, Fri–Sun 9.30–7
- 🚇 S-Bahn Tiergarten
- 🚌 Bus 100, 187, 341
- ♿ None
- 💷 Inexpensive
- ↔ Bauhaus-Archiv (► 36), Kulturforum (► 37)
- ❓ Viewing platform (no elevator)

The Siegessäule

39

Potsdamer Platz

INFORMATION

🔷 H6; Locator map E2
✉ Potsdamer Platz
🚇 S-Bahn or U-Bahn
   Potsdamer Platz
🚌 Bus 142, 148, 248, 348
🎫 Free
↔ Checkpoint Charlie
   (▶ 42), Topographie des
   Terrors (▶ 57),
   Kulturforum (▶ 37)

*A remaining section
of the Berlin Wall in·
Potsdamer Platz*

This redeveloped business district is constantly expanding and is rapidly becoming a modern cultural hot spot. Restaurants, cafés, bars, cinemas and shops surround the cupola of the Sony Center to the north and the Arkaden shopping complex (▶ 72) to the south.

Rebuiding Bombing raids during World War II destroyed almost all of the 19th-century buildings in Potsdamer Platz, once the bustling heart of the city. During the years of division, the wall between East and West Berlin ran right through the middle of the square—look out for the line of metal plaques imbedded in the street paving, marking where the wall once stood. Few buildings remained standing after years of conflict. Investors have only managed to finance the reconstruction of a few of the old buildings such as the glass covered Kaisersaal, now a gourmet restaurant (▶ 64), in the Sony Center. Between 1993 and 1998 more than 100 cranes were brought into Potsdamer Platz, making it Europe's largest inner city building site. Shiny skyscrapers now dominate the skyline.

The Sony Center Designed by Helmut Jahn and built between 1996 and 2000, the Sony Center is one of Berlin's most impressive architectural attractions. The steel and glass dome measures 4,013sq m (43,195sq ft) and shelters the gleaming office buildings, shops, cinemas, alfresco dining establishments and central piazza beneath.

Film Movie buffs will have plenty to keep them occupied. There are three multiplex cinemas to choose from, including two 3-D Imax theatres and an art house cinema in the Filmhaus underneath the Berlin Film Museum (▶ 52).

Brandenburger Tor

The Brandenburg Gate began life as a humble toll-gate, marking the city's western boundary. Today it symbolizes the reconciliation of East and West and is the perfect backdrop for commemorative events, celebrations and pop concerts.

Gate of Peace? The gate is the work of Karl Gotthard Langhans and dates from 1788–91. Its neoclassical style echoes the ancient entrance to the Acropolis in Athens, on which it is modelled. Conceived as an Arch of Peace, the Brandenburg Gate has more frequently been used to glorify martial values, as in 1933, when the Nazis' torchlight procession through the arch was intended to mark the beginning of the 1,000-year Reich.

Viktoria *The Quadriga*, a sculpture depicting the goddess Viktoria driving her chariot, was added to the gate by Johann Gottfried Schadow in 1794. In 1806, following the Prussian defeat at Jena, it was moved to Paris by Napoleon. When it was brought back in triumph less than a decade later, Karl Friedrich Schinkel added a wreath of oak leaves and the original iron cross to Viktoria's standard. During the heyday of cabaret in the 1920s, *The Quadriga* was often parodied by scantily clad chorus girls.

Pariser Platz During Berlin's booming 1990s, the adjoining square was transformed. Noteworthy buildings include the Adlon Hotel, the Academy of Arts and the DG Bank.

HIGHLIGHTS

- *The Quadriga*
- Classical reliefs
- Adjoining classical pavilions
- View down Unter den Linden
- View down Strasse des 17 Juni
- 'Room of Silence' (in pavilion)
- Pariser Platz
- Tourist office and shop

The Quadriga

INFORMATION

- ✚ H5; Locator map E2
- ✉ Pariser Platz
- 🚇 S-Bahn Unter den Linden, U-Bahn Französische Strasse
- 🚌 Bus 100, 147, 248, 257, 348
- 🚉 Friedrichstrasse
- ♿ None
- 🎫 Free

Checkpoint Charlie

HIGHLIGHTS

- Memorial to Wall victim
- Four-language sign
- Portraits of US and Soviet soldiers
- Sentry box

Haus am Checkpoint Charlie
- Isetta car
- Hot-air balloon

INFORMATION

- ⊞ J6; Locator map E2
- ✉ Friedrichstrasse 43–45
- ☎ 030 253 72 50
- 🕐 Daily 9am–10pm
- Ⓤ U-Bahn Kochstrasse, Stadtmitte
- 🚌 Bus 129
- 🚃 Yorckstrasse
- ♿ Few
- 💷 Expensive
- ↔ Potsdamer Platz (▶ 40)

Berlin will be famous for its Wall long after Berliners have consigned it to memory. The exhibition in the Haus am Checkpoint Charlie offers a colourful, if highly commercialized, presentation of the Wall experience.

Confrontation It was at this former border crossing that Soviet and US tanks faced off following the construction of the Wall in August 1961. The original prefabricated sentry box has been replaced with a replica, complete with sandbags and two idealized portraits of US and Soviet servicemen by artist Frank Thiel. A multilingual sign warns: 'You are leaving the American sector'.

Redevelopment Teams of international architects have been drafted to redesign the former no-man's land with instructions to merge the eastern and western parts of the city. New landmarks include the Business Centre by Philip Johnson, the Triangle by Josef Kleihues and the tower block commissioned by GSW (Partnership for Housing Development). Across the road is a lone remnant of 19th-century Berlin, a pharmacy-turned-café known as At the White Eagle.

Haus am Checkpoint Charlie Popular with young people generally, the museum is often crowded. On display are adapted vehicles, trick suitcases and a hot-air balloon used for escapes to the West. This emphasis on the sensational sits uncomfortably with the museum's stated purpose, which is to explore the Wall's human rights implications. To this end, there are exhibitions on the Wall's history, on painters and graffiti artists, and on the non-violent struggle for human rights, from Gandhi to Lech Walesa.

Gendarmenmarkt

This beautiful square comes as a pleasant surprise for visitors who associate Berlin with imperial bombast and Prussian marching bands. Climb the Französischer Dom tower for superb views of the Friedrichstadt.

Konzerthaus Known originally as the Schauspielhaus (theatre), the Konzerthaus was designed by Karl Friedrich Schinkel in 1821. Its predecessor was destroyed by fire during a rehearsal of Schiller's play *The Robbers*, so it is fitting that the playwright's monument stands outside (▶ 60). When the building was restored in the early 1980s after being severely damaged in World War II, the original stage and auditorium were dispensed with to make way for a concert hall with a capacity of 1,850—hence the change of name. The façade, however, retains Schinkel's original design. Keep an eye out for the sculpture of Apollo in his chariot.

Two cathedrals The twin French and German cathedrals (Französischer Dom and Deutscher Dom) occupy opposite ends of the square. The architect Karl von Gontard was described as an ass by Frederick the Great; one of the complementary cupolas collapsed in 1781. A small museum in the Deutscher Dom charts the history of German democracy from the 19th century to the present with photographs, film and a variety of artefacts. A museum in the Französischer Dom tells the story of the hardworking Huguenots who settled in Berlin in the 17th century, fleeing persecution in France. The Cathedral (minus its baroque tower, a later addition) was built for them. The cathedral's other attractions include the Turmstube restaurant in the tower, and the famous carillon, which plays three times daily.

HIGHLIGHTS

- Konzerthaus
- Statue of Schiller
- Apollo in his chariot
- Deutscher Dom
- Cathedrals' twin towers

Französischer Dom
- Turmstube
- Balustrade view
- Carillon

Konzerthaus

INFORMATION

www.franzoesischer-dom-berlin.de

- ✚ J5; Locator map E2
- ☎ Französischer Dom: 030 02 29 17 60. Deutscher Dom: 030 22 73 04 31
- ◉ Französischer Dom: daily 9–7. Huguenot Museum: Tue–Sat noon–5, Sun 11–5. Deutscher Dom: Tue 10am–11pm, Wed 10–6
- Ⓠ U-Bahn Stadtmitte, Französische Strasse,
- 🚌 Bus 100, 147, 257, 348
- 🚉 Friedrichstrasse
- 💶 Inexpensive

43

Unter den Linden

HIGHLIGHTS

- Deutsche Staatsoper
- Façade of Alte-Königliche Bibliothek
- Statue of Frederick the Great
- Humboldt University
- Neue Wache
- Zeughaus (note especially the masks of dying warriors in the Schlüterhof)
- Cannon (in the Schlüterhof)
- Opernpalais Unter den Linden Café (➤ 71)
- Hedwigskirche

INFORMATION

- ✚ J5; Locator map E2
- ✉ Unter den Linden 2
- ☎ Deutsches Historisches Museum (German History Museum): 030 20 30 40. Hedwigskirche: 030 203 48 10
- 🕐 Deutsches Historisches Museum: Thu–Tue 10–6. Hedwigskirche: Mon–Sat 10–5, Sun 12.30–5
- 🍴 Opernpalais Unter den Linden Café
- Ⓢ S-Bahn Unter den Linden, U-Bahn Französische Strasse
- 🚌 Bus 100
- 🚋 Friedrichstrasse
- ♿ None
- 💰 Deutsches Historisches Museum: inexpensive

The street 'Under the Linden Trees' —once the heart of imperial Berlin— boasts some fine neoclassical and baroque buildings. The pièce de résistance is Andreas Schlüter's superb sculptures of dying warriors in the courtyard of the Zeughaus.

Forum Fridericianum Frederick the Great presides over the eastern end of Unter den Linden. His equestrian statue, by Daniel Christian Rauch, stands next to Bebelplatz, once known as the Forum Fridericianum and intended by the Prussian monarch to evoke the grandeur of Imperial Rome. Dominating the square is Georg von Knobelsdorff's opera house, the Deutsche Staatsoper. Facing it is the Old Royal Library (Alte-Königliche Bibliothek), completed in 1780 and nicknamed the Kommode (chest of drawers) by quick-witted Berliners. Here, in 1933, Nazi propaganda chief Josef Goebbels consigned the works of ideological opponents to the flames in a public book-burning. Just south of Bebelplatz is the Roman Catholic cathedral, the Hedwigskirche, whose classical lines echo the Pantheon in Rome.

Zeughaus Frederick's civic project was never completed, but the buildings on the opposite side of Unter den Linden keep up imperial appearances. Karl Marx was a student at the Humboldt University, designed by Johann Boumann as a palace for Frederick the Great's brother in 1748. Next comes the Neue Wache (Guardhouse), which Schinkel designed in 1818 to complement Johann Nering's magnificent 1695 baroque palace, the Zeughaus (Arsenal). The Deutsches Historisches Museum (German History Museum) moved back to the Kronprinzenpalais opposite early in 2004.

Museumsinsel

Berlin's famed collection of antiquities, dispersed during World War II, is one of the city's major treasures. To see it, head for Museums Island, accessible over the Monbijou Bridge, in the Spree. The Pergamon (► 46) is one of five superb institutions there.

Altes Museum Built in 1830, this was the first museum on the island. Karl Schinkel's magnificent classical temple shares with the Pergamon (► 46) fabulous collections of sculptures, paintings and artefacts from all corners of the ancient world. The building itself accorded with Schinkel's vision of Berlin as Athens on the Spree. The impression made by the façade is overwhelming, and hidden at the core of the building is a rotunda inspired by Rome's Pantheon and lined with statues of the gods.

Neues Museum Beginning in 2009 Berlin's famed Egyptian collections will be housed once again in this museum, designed in 1843 by August Stüler. Treasures include the bust of Queen Nefertiti currently in the Egyptian Museum (► 52); she may be reunited with a similar bust of her husband, King Akhenaten.

Bode-Museum Named after Wilhelm von Bode (1845–1929), for 20 years curator of Museums Island, this 1904 building will exhibit exquisite medieval sculptures (including works by German master Tilman Riemenschneider), early Christian and Byzantine art, and a superb coin collection. Scheduled to reopen in 2006.

Alte Nationalgalerie This gallery displays mainly paintings of the 19th century, and includes works by Impressionists such as Manet, Monet, Degas and Cézanne.

HIGHLIGHTS

- View of Altes Museum from the Lustgarten
- Rotunda of Altes Museum
- *Unter den Linden*, Franz Krüger (Alte Nationalgalerie)
- *Portrait of Frederick the Great at Potsdam*, Adolph Menzel (Alte Nationalgalerie)
- View from Monbijou Bridge

INFORMATION

www.smpk.de
- J5; Locator map D1
- Museumsinsel
- 030 20 90 55 55 (info)
- While rebuilding continues, some museums are open only for temporary exhibitions Tue–Sun 10–6
- S-Bahn Hackescher Markt, U- and S-Bahn Friedrichstrasse
- Bus 100, 157, 200, 348
- Hackescher Markt
- Few
- Moderate
- Pergamon Museum (► 46), Berliner Dom (► 47)

Schinkel's Rotunda, the Altes Museum

45

Pergamon Museum

HIGHLIGHTS

- 120m (394ft) frieze on Pergamon Altar
- Market gate from Miletus
- Ishtar Gate
- Façade of Mshatta Palace
- Nebuchadnezzar's throne room
- Figurines from Jericho
- Panelled room from Aleppo
- Bust of the Emperor Caracalla
- Statue of Aphrodite from Myrina
- Mosaic from Hadrian's villa at Tivoli

INFORMATION

www.smpk.de

- J5; Locator map D1
- Am Kupfergraben, Museumsinsel
- 030 20 90 55 55 (info)
- Tue–Sun 10–6. Thu 10–10
- Café
- S-Bahn Hackescher Markt
- Bus 100, 157, 200, 348
- Hackescher Markt
- Few
- Moderate
- Unter den Linden
  (► 44), Museumsinsel
  (► 45), Berliner Dom
  (► 47)

If you have time to visit only one museum in Berlin, choose the Pergamon. Virtually every corner of the ancient world is represented, from the Roman Empire to the Islamic world.

Controversy Like the other museums on Museums Island (Museumsinsel), the Pergamon was built to house the vast haul of antiquities amassed by German archaeologists in the 19th century. Controversy rages in museum circles over the proper home for such relics; some people argue that they were wrongfully plundered and have no place in Western museums.

Pergamon Altar The museum's most stunning exhibit is the famous Pergamon Altar from Asia Minor, a stupendous monument so huge that it needs a hall more than 15m (50ft) high to accommodate it. From Bergama on the west coast of Turkey, it was excavated by Carl Humann in 1878–86. Dating from about 164 BC, it was actually part of a complex of royal palaces, temples, a library and a theatre. Hardly less impressive is the reconstructed market gateway of Miletus, built by the Romans in this town in western Turkey in AD 120 during the reign of Emperor Hadrian. The Babylonian Ishtar Gate makes a startling contrast with its brilliantly coloured bricks of glazed clay. Built between 604 and 562 BC, it was dedicated to the goddess of war, Ishtar, whose symbol was a lion.

Antiquities The museum also has a splendid collection of Greek and Roman statues (some of them retaining traces of their original vibrant colouring), Islamic art, figurines and clay tablets. Many more artefacts come from Sumeria and other parts of the Middle East.

Berliner Dom

For evidence of imperial pretensions, look to Berlin's Protestant cathedral. The cathedral's vast vault contains the sarcophagi of more than 90 members of the Hohenzollern dynasty.

Cathedral Architect Julius Raschdorff built the Berliner Dom over the site of a smaller imperial chapel. The existing cathedral was completed in 1905 and opened in the presence of Kaiser Wilhelm II. Inside, the most impressive feature is the 74m- (234ft-) high dome, supported by pillars of Silesian sandstone and decorated with mosaics of the Beatitudes by Anton von Werner. In High Renaissance style, its huge dome, open to the public and reached by climbing 270 steps, is reminiscent of St. Peter's in Rome. The cathedral was badly damaged during World War II, but restoration started in 1974 after years of neglect and is now well advanced. Work on the stained-glass windows has been completed.

Destroyed by Allied bombs The name of the square, Lustgarten, derives from the former pleasure garden which stood just outside the cathedral on Museumsinsel. The site, where the Great Elector is said to have planted potatoes, is now covered by grass and paving. Opposite, until the Allied bombings in World War II, stood the enormous Berliner Schloss, dating from the early 18th century and designed by Andreas Schlüter and Johann Eosander von Göethe. The statue of the Great Elector, now in front of Schloss Charlottenburg, once stood here. There has been a campaign to have the Berliner Schloss rebuilt. The cost, however, will surely be prohibitive.

HIGHLIGHTS

- Lustgarten
- High Renaissance-style façade
- Baptism chapel
- Imperial staircase
- Sarcophagi
- 74m- (234ft-) high dome
- Carved figures above altar
- Viewing gallery

INFORMATION

- ✚ K5; Locator map D1
- ✉ Am Lustgarten
- ☎ 030 20 26 91 19
- 🕐 Apr–end Sep Mon–Sat 9–8, Sun 12–8; Oct–Mar Mon–Sat 9–8, Sun 12–7
- 🍴 None
- Ⓤ U- and S-Bahn Alexanderplatz, S-Bahn Hackescher Markt
- 🚌 Bus 100, 157, 348
- 🚋 Hackescher Markt
- ♿ Few
- 💲 Moderate

The Dom from Marx-Engels-Forum

Nikolaiviertel

HIGHLIGHTS

Nikolaikirche
- Exhibition of Berlin history
- Gothic nave
- *The Good Samaritan*, Michael Ribestein
- Hunger Cloth (in vestry)
- Wooden *Crucifixion* of 1485

Nikolaiviertel
- Knoblauchhaus
- Ephraim-palais
- Zum Nussbaum (➤ 71)
- Well outside the pub Zum Paddenwirt

INFORMATION

www.stadtmuseum.de
- K5; Locator map E1
- Poststrasse
- Nikolaikirche: 03 24 72 45 29. Knoblauchhaus: 030 27 57 67 33. Ephraim-palais: 030 24 00 21 21
- Nikolaikirche: Tue–Sun 10–6 Knoblauchhaus: Tue–Sun 10–6 Ephraimpalais: Tue–Sun 10–6
- U- and S-Bahn Alexanderplatz
- Bus 100, 142, 157, 200, 257, 348
- Alexanderplatz
- Few
- Nikolaikirche: moderate Knoblauchhaus: moderate Ephraimpalais: moderate

Step back two or three centuries and enjoy a wander through the Nikolai Quarter, a diverting pastiche of baroque and neoclassical architecture, with rows of gabled houses, cobbled streets and quaint shops.

Nikolaikirche The dominating landmark is the twin-spired church that gives the Nikolaiviertel its name. The Nikolaikirche is the oldest church in Berlin, dating originally from 1200 although the present building was not completed until 1470. Seriously damaged in World War II, the beautifully proportioned Gothic nave has been sensitively restored. The church is of great historic importance, because it was here, in 1307, that the two communities of Berlin and Cölln were formally united. The church, now used for services only occasionally, houses a museum of Berlin history that includes models of the medieval city.

Around the Quarter Two other notable buildings recall the lavish lifestyle of Imperial Berlin. The pink stuccoed Knoblauchhaus was designed in 1759 by Friedrich Wilhelm Dietrichs for one of Berlin's most distinguished families. The family's history is illustrated in a small museum with paintings and Biedermeier furniture. The extravagant Ephraim-Palais in rococo style, with golden balconies and stone cherubs, once belonged to Frederick the Great's banker, Nathan Ephraim. The interior is decorated with art of the 17th to the 19th centuries.

Most picturesque Among streets, the title probably goes to Eiergasse and Am Nussbaum, named for its cheery reconstruction of a famous 16th-century Berlin inn, Zum Nussbaum ('At the Nut Tree')—a good refreshment stop.

Alexanderplatz

A victim of East German town planning, 'Alex' (as Berliners affectionately call this historic old market place) is waiting to be revamped by a new generation of architects with a mandate to return it to the people.

Historic square Alexanderplatz is named after Russian Tsar Alexander I, who once reviewed troops here. The square was colonized by Berlin's burgeoning working class in the middle of the 19th century. Crime flourished, so it is no accident that the police headquarters was near by.

TV tower The Fernsehturm rises like an unlovely flower from the centre of the square. Its single virtue is its great height, which at 362m (1,188ft) exceeds even that of Paris's Eiffel Tower. Climb it on a fine day for panoramic city views. The cost of Hans Kolhoff's ambitious plans for the eventual development of the square may be prohibitive.

Other attractions Two historic buildings add lustre to the edges of Alexanderplatz. City Hall was formerly known as the Rotes Rathaus (Red Town Hall) because of its colour. Architect Heinrich Friedrich Waesemann was inspired by the municipal architecture of Renaissance Italy when he designed the building in 1869. The Marienkirche, Berlin's second-oldest church, is a survivor from an earlier age. The nave is 15th-century, and the lantern tower a flight of fancy added by Karl Gotthard Langhans in 1790. An epidemic of the plague in 1484 is commemorated in a large medieval wall painting entitled *Totentanz* (*Dance of Death*).

HIGHLIGHTS

- Fernsehturm
- Rotes Rathaus
- World Time Clock
- Neptune Fountain
- Forum Hotel
- Kaufhof department store (► 72)
- Marienkirche
- *Totentanz* (*Dance of Death*) wall painting

Fernsehturm and City Hall

INFORMATION

- ✚ K5; Locator map D1
- ☎ Fernsehturm: 030 242 33 33. Marienkirche 030 242 44 67
- ◷ Fernsehturm: daily 9–12.30. Marienkirche: Mon–Thu 10–4, Sat noon–4
- 🍴 Cafés; Fernsehturm; Telecafé with view
- Ⓤ U- or S-Bahn Alexanderplatz
- 🚌 Bus 100, 157, 200, 348
- 🎟 Fernsehturm: moderate

49

Schloss Köpenick

HIGHLIGHTS

- Dutch baroque façade
- Stucco ceiling of the Wappensaal
- Collection of gold and silver tableware
- Swiss panelled room
- Jugendstil glass
- 18th-century furniture
- Baroque chapel
- Schlossinsel
- View of the old fishing port of Kietz

INFORMATION

- Off map to southeast; Locator map C1
- Schlossinsel
- Park: daily 6–9 (summer); 8–dusk (winter)
- Café   None
- S-Bahn Köpenick
- Bus 167, 169, 360
- Köpenick
- Free
- Palace Alt Köpenick 34
  ☎ 030 26 62 902

Standing in peaceful parkland on the Schlossinsel, at the confluence of the Dahme and Spree, this time-worn, 17th-century former residence of the rulers of the Mark Brandenburg has its own offbeat charm.

Royal residence The current Schloss, built in the Dutch baroque style by Rutger van Langefelt for Elector Friedrich in 1681, stands on the site of a 9th-century Slav fortress. Its most remarkable feature is the Hall of Arms (Wappensaal), whose stuccoed ceiling is by Italian artisan Giovanni Carove. Classical figures support the coats of arms of the Mark Brandenburg. The chapel, dating from 1682 to 1685, is a distinguished example of Arnold Nering's work.

Museum The Schloss also houses a branch of the Kunstgewerbemuseum (Museum of Applied Art ► 38). The display includes silverware rescued from the ruins of the Berlin Royal Palace at the end of World War II. There is furniture by David Roentgens, including an elegant cabinet dating from 1779, a small but fine collection of glassware, and a dinner service belonging to Frederick II, manufactured by the famous Royal Porcelain Factory.

Köpenick Köpenick was a hotbed of working-class resistance to the Nazis. More than 90 people perished during Blutwoche, the 'blood week' in 1933, and many others were imprisoned and tortured. A memorial in Puchanstrasse commemorates the events. Today the old town (Altstadt) is undergoing extensive restoration. Its dilapidated but picturesque streets, dating from the 13th century, retain an antique flavour and are worth exploring.

The Dutch baroque façade

BERLIN's
best

Museums *52–53*

Galleries *54*

Places of Worship *55*

Bridges *56*

Political Sights *57*

Parks & Gardens *58*

Views *59*

Statues & Monuments *60*

For Children *61*

What's Free *62*

Museums

CITY OF MUSEUMS

Berlin's museums are justifiably renowned the world over for their comprehensiveness and diversity. Many subjects still have two collections devoted to them—one from the East and one from the West. This situation arose amid the confusion of the divided city after World War II, when many of the artefacts were stolen or dispersed and had to be brought back together again. The fantastic archaeological finds of the 19th century, brought here by the cartload, make the museums specializing in antiquities a treat.

Bust of Queen Nefertiti, Egyptian Museum

In the Top 25

19 DEUTSCHES HISTORISCHES MUSEUM (GERMAN HISTORY MUSEUM, ► 44)

7 ETHNOLOGISCHES MUSEUM (ETHNOLOGICAL MUSEUM), DAHLEM (► 32)

17 HAUS AM CHECKPOINT CHARLIE (CHECKPOINT CHARLIE MUSEUM, ► 42)

18 HISTORICAL EXHIBITION IN DEUTSCHER DOM (► 43)

18 HUGENOTTENMUSEUM (HUGUENOT MUSEUM), IN FRANZÖSISCHER DOM (► 43)

13 KUNSTGEWERBEMUSEUM (MUSEUM OF APPLIED ART), KULTURFORUM (► 38)

12 MUSIKINSTRUMENTEN-MUSEUM (MUSEUM OF MUSICAL INSTRUMENTS), KULTURFORUM (► 37)

21 PERGAMON MUSEUM (► 46)

ÄGYPTISCHES MUSEUM (EGYPTIAN MUSEUM)

The undisputed star of this rich collection is the bust of Tutankhamen's aunt, Queen Nefertiti, dating from about 1340 BC. There are also mummies, death masks, jewellery and even games.

C5 ✉ Schlossstrasse 70 ☎ 030 20 90 55 55 ⏰ Tue–Sun 10–6 🚌 Bus 109, 145, 210, X21 🚇 U-Bahn Sophie-Charlotte-Platz ✋ Moderate

BRÖHAN MUSEUM

In 1983, Professor Karl Bröhan presented his superb collection of Jugendstil and art deco crafts to the city. The highlight of the museum are the rooms decorated in the styles of the leading designers of the period.

B5 ✉ Schlossstrasse 1a ☎ 030 32 69 06 00 ⏰ Tue–Sun 10–6 🚌 Bus 109, 145, 210, X26 🚇 U-Bahn Sophie-Charlotte-Platz ✋ Moderate

DEUTSCHES TECHNIKMUSEUM (GERMAN TECHNOLOGY MUSEUM)

A thoroughly entertaining and beautifully presented exhibition in the locomotive sheds of the old Anhalter train station. Everything from biplanes and vintage cars to model ships and computers.

H7 ✉ Trebbiner Strasse 9 ☎ 030 90 25 40 ⏰ Tue–Fri 9–5.30, Sat–Sun 10–6 🚇 U-Bahn Gleisdreieck 🚌 Bus 129, 248 ✋ Moderate

FILMMUSEUM BERLIN (FILM MUSEUM)

A fascinating journey through the history of German film from 1895. Includes a special tribute to Marlene Dietrich.

H6 ✉ Potsdamer Strasse 2 ☎ 030 30 09 030 ⏰ Tue–Sun 10–6, Thu 10–8 🚇 U- or S-Bahn Potsdamer Platz ✋ Moderate

JÜDISCHES MUSEUM (JEWISH MUSEUM)

This controversial new building by Polish-born architect, Daniel Libeskind, contains an exhibition on German–Jewish history from the earliest times to the present day.

✚ J7 ⊠ Lindenstrasse 9–14 ☎ 030 25 99 33 00 ⏱ Tue–Sun 10–8, Mon 10–10 🚇 U-Bahn Kochstrasse 👤 Moderate

German Technology Museum

MÄRKISCHES MUSEUM

The museum's permanent exhibition traces the cultural history of Berlin from the Middle Ages to the present day. Highlights include the one remaining original horse's head from the Brandenburg Tor *quadriga* (➤ 41) and an unusual collection of self-playing musical machines.

✚ K6 ⊠ Am Köllnischen Park 5 ☎ 030 30 86 60 ⏱ Tue–Sun 10–6 🚇 U-Bahn Märkisches Museum 🚌 Bus 143, 147, 240, 265 👤 Moderate

MUSEUM FÜR INDISCHE KUNST; OSTASIATISCHE KUNST (MUSEUMS OF INDIAN & EAST ASIAN ART)

Two museums within a complex of galleries in Dahlem, presenting the art and culture of India and the Far East with style and imagination.

✚ Off map to south ⊠ Lansstrasse 8 ☎ 030 20 90 55 55 ⏱ Tue–Fri 10–6, Sat–Sun 11–6 🚇 U-Bahn Dahlem-Dorf 👤 Inexpensive

MUSEUM FÜR NATURKUND (NATURAL HISTORY MUSEUM)

Explore the 6,000sq m (64, 585sq ft) of museum space filled with geology, palaeontology and zoology exhibits, plus the largest assembled dinosaur skeleton in the world.

✚ H4 ⊠ Invalidenstrasse 43 ☎ 030 20 93 85 91 ⏱ Tue–Fri 9.30–5, Sat, Sun 10–6 🚇 U-Bahn Zinnowitzer Strasse, S-Bahn Nordbahnhof 👤 Moderate

SAMMLUNG INDUSTRIELLE GESTALTUNG

East German design from the 1950s to the present day—industrial design, advertising and packaging.

✚ L3 ⊠ Knaackstrasse 97 ☎ 030 44 31 78 68 ⏱ Wed–Sun 1–8 🚇 U-Bahn Eberswalder Strasse 👤 Inexpensive

THE STORY OF BERLIN

This state-of-the-art exhibition uses 3-D sound systems, touch screens, time tunnels and adventure rooms to tell the story of Berlin since 1237.

✚ E7 ⊠ Kufürstendamm 207–208, Ku'damm Karree ☎ 030 88 72 01 00 ⏱ Daily 10–8 🚇 U-Bahn Kufürstendamm 🚌 Bus 109, 119, 129, 219, 249 👤 Expensive (family card available)

TROY'S TREASURES

Rumours abound concerning the return of Berlin's most famous archaeological treasure, the 10,000 objects recovered by Heinrich Schliemann from the site of what he assumed to be the ancient city of Troy in the 1870s. Rather fancifully, as it turned out, Schliemann attributed the vast hoard of gold to the Homeric hero King Priam himself. The collection disappeared during World War II, but has since been on show in Moscow.

Galleries

DIE BRÜCKE

Anyone wishing for an introduction to 20th-century art could hardly do better than visit the Brücke Museum on the edge of the Grunewald forest. The artistic movement known as Die Brücke (the Bridge), which flourished between 1905 and 1913, was in the vanguard of German Expressionism. The landscapes and portraits by Ludwig Kirchner, Karl Schmidt-Rottluff, Emil Nolde, Max Pechstein and others bridge the gap between figurative and abstract art and make Cubism more comprehensible.

In the Top 25

🔟 **BAUHAUS-ARCHIV (BAUHAUS MUSEUM, ► 36)**

🔢 **EPHRAIM-PALAIS (► 48)**

🔢 **GEMÄLDEGALERIE (PICTURE GALLERY), KULTURFORUM (► 37)**

9️⃣ **KÄTHE-KOLLWITZ-MUSEUM (► 34)**

🔢 **ALTE NATIONALGALERIE (► 45)**

🔢 **NEUE NATIONALGALERIE (NEW NATIONAL GALLERY), KULTURFORUM (► 37)**

BRÜCKE MUSEUM

This gallery exhibits work from the group of 20th-century German artists known as Die Brücke.

➕ Off map to south ✉ Bussardsteig 9 ☎ 030 831 20 29 🕐 Wed–Mon 11–5 🚌 Bus 115 💶 Moderate

EASTSIDE GALLERY

Graffiti art as revealed on 730m (2,395ft) of the former Berlin Wall, on the north bank of the River Spree. It is said to be the world's largest open-air art gallery.

➕ M6 ✉ Mühlenstrasse 🚇 U- and S-Bahn Warschauer Strasse 🚌 Bus 140, 142, 147, 340 💶 Free

HAMBURGER BAHNHOF

The Hamburger Bahnhof, the oldest station in Berlin, has been converted into a spacious modern art gallery.

➕ G4 ✉ Invalidenstrasse 50–51 ☎ 030 39 78 34 12 🕐 Tue–Fri 10–6, Sat, Sun 11–6 🚇 S-Bahn Hauptbahnhof, Lehrter Bahnhof 💶 Moderate

*The Rotunda of
Sammlung Berggruen*

KUPFERSTICH-KABINETT

The 'engravings room' is a collection of drawings and prints by some of the great European artists, including Cranach, Dürer, Pieter Bruegel the Elder, Rembrandt and Kandinsky.

➕ G6 ✉ Matthäikirchplatz 6 ☎ 030 20 90 55 55 🕐 Tue–Fri 10–6 🚇 U- or S-Bahn Potsdamer Platz 💶 Inexpensive

SAMMLUNG BERGGRUEN

A stimulating exhibition of paintings and sculptures by Picasso and his contemporaries. There are nearly 70 pieces by Picasso, as well as works by Klee, Braque, Giacometti and Cézanne.

➕ B5 ✉ Schlossstrasse 1 ☎ 030 20 90 55 55 🕐 Tue–Fri 10–6, Sat, Sun 11–6 🚇 U-Bahn Sophie-Charlotte-Platz 🚌 Bus 109, 145, 210, X21 💶 Moderate

Places of Worship

In the Top 25

22 BERLINER DOM (BERLIN CATHEDRAL, ➤ 47)
16 FRANZÖSISCHER DOM
(FRENCH CATHEDRAL, ➤ 43)
19 HEDWIGSKIRCHE (➤ 44)
10 KAISER-WILHELM-GEDÄCHTNISKIRCHE
(KAISER WILHELM MEMORIAL CHURCH, ➤ 35)
24 MARIENKIRCHE (➤ 49)
23 NIKOLAIKIRCHE (➤ 48)

K. F. SCHINKEL

No man left more of an impression on the architecture of Berlin than Karl Friedrich Schinkel (1781–1840). He favoured the classical style, as in the Konzerthaus (formerly the Schauspielhaus) and the Neue Wache. But in designing the Friedrichwerdersche Kirche he turned for inspiration to medieval Gothic. The beautifully proportioned nave is the setting for a satisfying exhibition on his life's work.

FRIEDRICHWERDERSCHE KIRCHE

Berlin's celebrated architect Karl Friedrich Schinkel designed this church in neo-Gothic style in 1824. It is now a museum honouring his work.

☩ J5 ☒ Werderscher Mark ☎ 030 208 13 23 ⏲ Tue–Sun 10–6 ⬛ U-Bahn Hausvogteiplatz ▣ Inexpensive

*Inside Friedrich-
werdersche Kirche*

GETHSEMANE KIRCHE

This church shot to fame overnight in 1989 when it became the spiritual centre of the resistance movement to the East German Communist regime. Regular concerts are held here.

☩ L2 ☒ Stargarder Strasse 77 ☎ 030 44 28 50 for services ⬛ U- or S-Bahn Schönhauser Allee

NEUE SYNAGOGE (NEW SYNAGOGUE)

The stunning dome of this 1866 building is one of Berlin's landmarks. Designed by Eduard Knoblauch and August Stüler, it survived the infamous Kristallnacht on 9 November 1938, when the Nazis destroyed Jewish buildings.

☩ J4 ☒ Oranienburger Strasse 28–30 ☎ 030 88 02 83 16 ⏲ Sun–Thu 10–5.30, Fri 10–1.30 ⬛ S-Bahn Oranienburger Strasse

SOPHIENKIRCHE

Berlin's sole surviving baroque church, completed in 1734, was designed by J. F. Grael.

☩ K4 ☒ Grosse Hamburger Strasse 29 ☎ 030 308 79 20 ⏲ May–Oct Wed 3–6, Sun 10 (service) ⬛ U-Bahn Weinmeisterstrasse

Bridges

┌─ **In the Top 25**
│ **3** GLIENICKER BRÜCKE (▶ 28)
│ **20** MONBIJOUBRÜCKE (▶ 45)

ROSA LUXEMBURG

The most dramatic event to occur at one of Berlin's many bridges was the recovery of the body of communist agitator Rosa Luxemburg in January 1919. After her murder by right-wing army officers in the Tiergarten, her corpse was dumped into the Landwehrkanal. It was found weeks later under the Lichtensteinbrücke.

FRIEDRICHS-BRÜCKE
This elegant bridge, built in 1892, provides a fine view of the Berliner Dom.
➕ K5 ✉ Bodestrasse 🚇 S-Bahn Hackescher Markt

GERTRAUDENBRÜCKE
Gertraud was a favourite saint of the fisherfolk who used to ply the waters here in the Middle Ages. Bronze water rats decorate the base of her statue.
➕ K6 ✉ Gertraudenstrasse 🚇 U-Bahn Spittelmarkt

JUNGFERNBRÜCKE
This drawbridge, dating from 1798, was once the haunt of Huguenot working girls selling silk and lace.
➕ K5 ✉ Friedrichsgracht 🚇 U-Bahn Spittelmarkt

LESSINGBRÜCKE
Gotthold Ephraim Lessing (1729–81) is one of Germany's best-known playwrights. Scenes from his dramas decorate the sandstone piers of 'his' bridge.
➕ F4 ✉ Lessingstrasse 🚇 U-Bahn Turmstrasse

MOABITER BRÜCKE
This bridge of 1864 is famous for the four bears that decorate it. The bear is the symbol of Berlin.
➕ F5 ✉ Bellevue Ufer 🚇 S-Bahn Bellevue

MOLTKEBRÜCKE
Named for a hero of the Franco-Prussian war, this belligerent bridge is guarded by Prussian eagles and cherubs wielding swords, spears, trumpets and drums. It was completed in 1891.
➕ G5 ✉ Willi-Brandt-Strasse 🚇 S-Bahn Lehrter Stadtbahnhof

OBERBAUMBRÜCKE
Over 500 different kinds of tiles were used in the renovation of what was once Berlin's longest bridge.
➕ N7 ✉ Mühlenstrasse 🚇 U-Bahn Schlesisches Tor

SCHLEUSENBRÜCKE
This simple iron bridge is decorated with historic scenes of Berlin.
➕ K5 ✉ Werderstrasse 🚇 U-Bahn Hausvogteiplatz

SCHLOSSBRÜCKE
Karl Friedrich Schinkel designed a new bridge to replace the decrepit Hundebrücke in 1819. Named after a royal palace that no longer exists, it is decorated with statues of Greek gods.
➕ K5 ✉ Unter den Linden 🚇 U-Bahn Hausvogteiplatz

Moltkebrücke

Political Sights

┌─ In the Top 25 ──────────────
16 BRANDENBURGER TOR
(BRANDENBURG GATE ➤ 41)
17 CHECKPOINT CHARLIE (➤ 42)
6 SACHSENHAUSEN (➤ 31)
└──────────────────────────────

GEDENKSTÄTTE HAUS DER WANNSEE KONFERENZ (WANNSEE CONFERENCE CENTRE)

In this innocuous-looking mansion on the shores of Lake Wannsee, leading Nazis plotted the mass extermination of Europe's 11 million Jews. The exhibition tells the whole horrific story.

🔢 Off map to southwest ✉ Am Grossen Wannsee 58–58 ☎ 030 805 00 10 🕐 Daily 10–6 🚇 S-Bahn Wannsee 🚌 Bus N114 💵 Free

REICHSTAG

The German parliament building, designed by Paul Wallot in 1884, has had a troubled but colourful history. The inscription on the façade, 'For the German people' was added during World War I. The Reichstag was the focus of the Battle for Berlin in 1945 and by the time Russian soldiers hoisted the Soviet flag the building was a smoking ruin. Fifty years later, restoration was entrusted to British architect Sir Norman Foster. The modern design was completed in 1999 prior to parliament's move from Bonn to Berlin. Although the new design preserved the shell of the building, the interior was gutted to create a new parliamentary chamber. Guided tours of the chamber must be pre-booked but access to the spectacular glass dome and viewing gallery are unrestricted so it is best to arrive early.

🔢 H5 ✉ Platz der Republik 1 ☎ 030 22 73 21 52 🕐 Daily 8am–midnight 🚇 S-Bahn Unter den Linden 🚌 Bus 100 💵 Free

FEDERAL CHANCELLERY

The Reichstag has a new neighbour. Across Platz der Republik a gleaming white block has been built to provide 370 offices for Chancellor Gerhard Schröder, his team of officials and political assistants. The new Federal Chancellery (Bundeskanzleramt) has been criticized for being too monumental. A few hundred metres away stands Schloss Bellevue, the official residence of Federal President Johannes Rau.

The Reichstag

TOPOGRAPHIE DES TERRORS

The Topography of Terror is an open-air exhibition in the excavations of the former National Socialist government district revealing the development and activities of the National Socialist SS and Police State. A new building to house the Foundation's International Documentation and Study Center, designed by the Swiss architect Peter Zumthor, is due to open in 2005.

🔢 H6 ✉ Niederkirchnerstrasse 8 ☎ 030 25 48 67 03 🕐 May–Sep daily 10–dusk; Oct–Apr daily 10–8 🚇 U- or S-Bahn Potsdamer Platz 🚌 Bus 129, 248, 341 💵 Free

Parks & Gardens

In the Top 25

14 TIERGARTEN (▶ 39)

BOTANISCHER GARTEN (BOTANICAL GARDEN)

More than 18,000 varieties of plants and flowers in beautifully landscaped grounds.

➕ Off map to south ✉ Königin-Luise-Strasse 6–8 ☎ 030 83 85 01 00 ⏰ Daily May–Oct 9–6; Nov–Apr 9–4 🚇 U-Bahn Rathaus Steglitz 🎫 Moderate

BRITZER GARTEN

Created for the National Garden Show in 1985, the 100-ha (247-acre) site is a favourite with cyclists, dog owners and families. There is a lake, nature trails and a restaurant.

➕ Off map to south ✉ Sangerhauser Weg 1 ☎ 030 700 90 60 ⏰ Summer: daily 9–8. Winter: daily 9–4 🚌 Bus 144, 179, 181 🎫 Free

FREIZEITPARK TEGEL

Possibly Berlin's best park—certainly its best for children—with table tennis, rowing, trampolines, volleyball, pedal boats and chess. Pleasure cruisers depart from the Greenwich promenade near by.

➕ Off map to northwest ✉ An der Malche 🚇 U-Bahn Alt-Tegel

The Botanical Garden

GREEN BERLIN

Flying over Berlin, every visitor is struck by the forest and lakes around the city, from Wannsee and the Grunewald in the west to Müggelsee and the Spreewald in the east. The city itself is unusually well provided with municipal parks—on hot Sunday afternoons they are Berliners' favourite spot.

TIERPARK BERLIN-FRIEDRICHSFELDE

One of Berlin's two zoos, located on the east side of the city in grounds that once formed part of Schloss Friedrichsfelde. Concerts and other events are held regularly in the restored palace.

➕ Off map to east ✉ Am Tierpark 125 ☎ 030 51 53 10 ⏰ Daily 9–dark 🚇 U-Bahn Tierpark

TREPTOWER PARK

The largest green space on the eastern side of the city spreads out along the banks of the River Spree. Fairs and other entertainments are often held here.

➕ N8 ✉ Puschkinallee 🚇 S-Bahn Treptower Park

VIKTORIAPARK

Best known for Karl Friedrich Schinkel's *Monument to the Wars of Liberation* (1813–15), this park can be approached from a row of terraces and gardens. There are good views of Berlin from the summit of the park. Children's playground.

➕ H8 ✉ Kreuzbergstrasse 🚇 U-Bahn Platz der Luftbrücke

VOLKSPARK JUNGFERNHEIDE

This park, on the northern edge of Charlottenburg, offers swimming, boat rental, hiking, sports fields and a theatre.

➕ B2 ✉ Saatwinkler Damm 🚇 U-Bahn Siemensdamm

Views

In the Top 25

24 FERNSEHTURM (► 49)
18 FRANZÖSISCHER DOM (► 43)
5 GRUNEWALDTURM (► 30)
4 JULIUSTURM, SPANDAU (► 29)
14 SIEGESSÄULE ► (39)

BERLIN HI-FLYER AT POTSDAMER PLATZ

A huge helium balloon is secured to the ground, rising up to a height of 150m (492ft), providing spectacular views across central Berlin.

➕ H6 ✉ Potsdamer Platz ☎ 030 69 51 37 30; 0180 5 708 708 🕐 Daily 10–8; restaurant 11–11 🚇 S- and U-Bahn Potsdamer Platz 🚌 Bus 148, 200, 348, TXL 💷 Expensive

EUROPA-CENTER (► 79)

FUNKTURM

Berlin's broadcasting tower was built between 1924 and 1926 to a design by Heinrich Straumer.

➕ A6 ✉ Messedamm ☎ 030 30 38 19 05 🕐 Summer: Sun–Thu 10–10, Fri, Sat 10am–midnight. Winter: Sun–Thu 11–6, Fri, Sat 11–7; restaurant 11–11 🚇 U-Bahn Kaiserdam 💷 Moderate

MÜGGELTURM

A 30m- (100ft-) high tower by the Teufelsee with views of the lake and woodlands of the Müggelsee. There is no lift so be prepared for a climb.

➕ Off map to southeast ✉ Kleiner Müggelberg ☎ 030 656 98 12 🕐 Daily 8am–dusk 🚌 Bus 169 💷 Inexpensive

OLYMPIASTADION (OLYMPIC STADIUM)

The 77m- (253ft-) high bell tower (*glockenturm*) of the Olympic Stadium affords excellent views of the Waldbühne, the Grunewald and the River Havel.

➕ Off map to west ✉ Am Glockenturm Olympische Platz ☎ 030 30 06 33; guided tours 030 30 11 10 113 🚇 S- and U-Bahn Olympiastadion 💷 Inexpensive

PANORAMA

In the Daimler Chrysler building you can take a ride in the fastest elevator in Europe. It takes only takes 20 second to reach the 100m- (328ft-) high viewing platform.

➕ Off map to west ✉ Am Glockenturm Olympische Platz ☎ 030 30 06 33; guided tours 030 30 11 10 113 🚇 S- and U-Bahn Olympiastadion 💷 Inexpensive

THE FUNKTURM

City wits nicknamed Berlin's broadcasting tower the Langer Lulatsch (Bean Pole). A symbol of German technical prowess at the time that it was first erected, it bears a faint resemblance to the Eiffel Tower in Paris. The restaurant is at a mere 55m (180ft), so if you plan to have a meal there, first take the lift up to the 126m- (413ft-) high viewing platform, overlooking the Grunewald forest in one direction and western Berlin in the other.

View from the TV Tower in Berlin showing Museum Island and the Pergamon Museum

Statues & Monuments

In the Top 25

🔢 **SIEGESSÄULE (➤ 39)**
🔢 **STATUE OF FREDERICK THE GREAT (➤ 44)**

MARX AND ENGELS

Unlike the statue of Lenin at Platz der Vereinten Nationen, the monolithic bronze sculptures of Karl Marx and Friedrich Engels will probably survive if only because of their sheer bulk. Just after the Wall came down, a sharp-witted East Berliner spray-painted the plinth with an apology on their behalf: 'We're sorry, it's not our fault–maybe next time things will turn out better.'

GEDENKSTÄTTE DEUTSCHER WIDERSTAND (MEMORIAL TO GERMAN RESISTANCE)

The Bendlerblock, focus of the ill-fated conspiracy against Hitler on 20 July 1944, houses an exhibition on opposition to Hitler.

➕ G6 ✉ Stauffenbergstrasse 13 ☎ 030 26 99 50 00 🕐 Mon–Fri 9–6, Sat, Sun 10–6 🚇 U-Bahn Kurfürstenstrasse

HENRY MOORE SCULPTURE, HAUS DER KULTUREN DER WELT

The British artist Henry Moore designed several statues for Berlin. This one, *Large Butterfly*, 'flutters' over a shallow lake outside the Kongresshalle.

➕ G5 ✉ John-Foster-Dulles-Allee 🚇 S-Bahn Unter den Linden

KLEISTGRAB (KLEIST'S GRAVE)

In a secluded spot in Wannsee is the grave of the Romantic poet Heinrich von Kleist, who committed suicide here with his mistress in 1811.

➕ Off map to southwest ✉ Bismarck-strasse 🚇 S-Bahn Wannsee

Statues of Marx and Engels

MARX AND ENGELS

The two founders of Communism stand forlorn in a tawdry garden near Alexanderplatz.

➕ K5 ✉ Rathausstrasse
🚇 U-Bahn Alexanderplatz

MONUMENT TO THE WARS OF LIBERATION (➤ 58)

SCHILLER MONUMENT

In front of the Konzerthaus in the Gendarmenmarkt (➤ 43) is Reinhold Begas' monument to Schiller (1869). Removed by the Nazi's in the 1930s, it was reinstated in 1988. Schiller is mounted on a pedestal, surrounded by the allegorical figures of Poetry, Drama, Philosophy and History.

➕ J5 ✉ Gendarmenmarkt 🚇 U-Bahn Stadtmitte, Französische Strasse

SCHLOSSBRÜCKE (➤ 56)

SOWJETISCHES EHRENMAL (SOVIET WAR MEMORIAL)

A heavy-handed commemoration of the 20,000 soldiers of the Red Army who died liberating Berlin during World War II.

➕ H5 ✉ Strasse des 17 Juni 🚇 S-Bahn Unter den Linden

For Children

BLUB-BADEPARADIES
Ride the Crazy River and water rapids and then relax over a picnic in the beautiful gardens outside the city.

✚ Off map ✉ Buschkrugallee 64 ☎ 030 60 90 60
🕐 Daily 10–11 🚇 U-Bahn Grenzalle 🚌 Bus 141 💷 Expensive

FILMPARK BABELSBERG
Occupying the site of the old UFA studios where Marlene Dietrich began her career, this theme park, visited on a 5- to 6-hour tour, takes a behind-the-scenes look at movie stunts, special effects and more.

✚ Off map ✉ August-Bebel-Strasse 26–53 ☎ 0331 721 27 50
🕐 Mar, Apr, Oct, Nov daily 10–4, May–end Sep 10–6 🚇 S-Bahn Babelsberg 💷 Expensive

FREIZEITPARK TEGEL (► 58)

MONBIJOU PARK
This park, near Museums Island, has a playground and a splash pool for toddlers.

✚ J4 ✉ Oranienburger Strasse 🚇 S-Bahn Hackescher Markt

SEALIFE BERLIN
Take a ride through middle of this cylindrical domed aquarium in a glass elevator and travel into an underwater world full of tropical fish.

✚ K5 ✉ Karl-Liebknecht-Strasse 5/Spandauer Strasse ☎ 040 3600 5612 🕐 Daily 10–6 🚇 S-Bahn Hackescher Markt 🚌 Bus 100, 143, 148, 200, 348, TXL; tram 2, 3, 4, 5, 6 💷 Expensive

ZEISS-GROSS-PLANETARIUM
Berlin has three planetariums and observatories. This one gives special monthly shows for children.

✚ M2 ✉ Prenzlauer Allee 80 ☎ 030 42 18 45 12
🕐 Shows: Mon–Fri 9.30, 11; also afternoons on Wed, Sat, Sun
🚇 S-Bahn Prenzlauer Allee 💷 Expensive

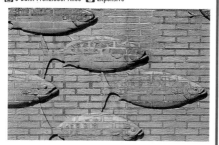

ZOOLOGISCHER GARTEN (ZOO AND AQUARIUM)
The more conveniently located of Berlin's two zoos.

✚ F6 ✉ Budapester Strasse ☎ 030 25 40 10 🕐 9–6.30 (aquarium 9–6) 🚇 U- or S-Bahn Zoologischer Garten 💷 Expensive

TRANSPORTATION AND TECHNOLOGY

The Deutsches Technikmuseum (German Technology Museum ► 52) is possibly the most child-orientated museum in Berlin. Its greatest attraction is that most of the displays are hands-on—there is even an experiment room where children can play with computers and other gadgets. The transport section covers everything from ox-carts to vintage cars while technology embraces printing presses, looms, street organs and much else besides.

A shoal of fish on the wall outside the zoo, in Budapester Strasse

THE DAHLEM CHRISTMAS MARKET

This market at Königin-Luise-Strasse 49 offers traditional arts and crafts, games for children and carriage rides to Grunewald.

What's Free

---In the Top 25---
🖪 **BATHING IN GRUNEWALD (▶ 30)**
🔟 **DEUTSCHES HISTORISCHES MUSEUM (GERMAN HISTORY MUSEUM, ▶ 44)**
🔟 **KAISER-WILHELM-GEDÄCHTNISKIRCHE (KAISER WILHELM MEMORIAL CHURCH, ▶ 35)**
🔟 **LISTENING TO BUSKERS ON BREITSCHEIDPLATZ (▶ 35)**
🔢 **ORGAN RECITALS IN BERLIN CATHEDRAL (▶ 47)**
🖪 **SACHSENHAUSEN (▶ 31)**
🔢 **TIERGARTEN (▶ 39)**

MONEYSAVERS

Wandering the streets and observing everyday life is the the best free entertainment in town. Most attractions have an admission charge, albeit usually a reasonable one, with reductions for children, students and senior citizens. Some museums offer free admission on Sundays and public holidays. There's no charge at Berlin's many parks (▶ 58) or at the various memorial museums, including the Gedenkstätte Deutscher Widerstand (▶ 60) and the Plötzensee Memorial. Many of the commercial art galleries (▶ 75) are also free.

BIKE RENTAL

Well, *almost* free…Biking is the cheapest way to get around quickly and pleasurably. Rent from **Fahrradstation** at:
➕ K4 ✉ Rosenthalerstrasse 40–1 🚇 S-Bahn Hackescher Markt
➕ J4 ✉ Auguststrasse 29a 🚇 S-Bahn Oranienburger Strasse
➕ J8 ✉ Bergmannstrasse 9 🚇 U-Bahn Gneisenaustrasse
☎ Central information and reservations number: 0180 5108000

INTERIOR OF WITTENBERGPLATZ
U-BAHN STATION

The 1920s art-deco booking hall has wooden ticket offices, original tiling, and period posters advertising cars and pianos.
➕ F7 ✉ Tauentzienstrasse 🚇 U-Bahn Wittenbergplatz

MAUERPARK

A long section of the former death strip of the Berlin Wall that was sprayed with artistic graffiti after 1989 and now documents Berlin's history since the fall of the wall.
➕ K3 ✉ Prenzlauer Berg
🚇 U-Bahn Bernauer Strasse, U-Bahn Eberswalder Strasse
🚌 Bus 120, 328

REICHSTAG (▶ 57)

VELOTAXI

Fun, inexpensive and eco-friendly, these three-wheeled bikes have an egg-shaped cabin with seats for two passengers and one rider. You can hail them in the street or
☎ 030 443 19 40

The Tiergarten, free and right in the middle of Berlin

WANNSEE–KLADOW FERRY

The enjoyable ferry ride from Wannsee to Kladow is inexpensive (free with a *Tageskarte* ▶ 91).
➕ Off map to southwest ✉ Wannsee Pier 🚌 BVG Line F10

BERLIN
where to...

EAT
German Restaurants *64*
Other European
    Restaurants *65–67*
International Restaurants *68–69*
Cafés *70–71*

SHOP
Department Stores &
    Souvenirs *72*
Boutiques & Designer Clothes *73*
Second-hand & Offbeat *74*
Galleries *75*
Home Furnishings &
    Accessories *76*
Markets & Food Shops *77*
The Best of the Rest *78–79*

BE ENTERTAINED
Theatres, Concerts &
    Cinemas *80*
Cabaret *81*
Pubs, Bars & Clubs *82–83*
Folk, Jazz & Rock *84*
Sport *85*

STAY
Luxury Hotels *86*
Mid-Range Hotels *87*
Budget Accommodation *88*

German Restaurants

PRICES

The restaurants in this section are in three categories shown by € signs. Expect to pay per person for a meal, excluding drink:

€   up to €13
€€   €13–€26
€€€   over €26

TRADITIONAL FARE

In Berlin plates come piled high with the two local staples, meat (usually pork) and potatoes, often accompanied by pickled cabbage (*Sauerkraut*), peas and the ubiquitous pickle. *Buletten* (meatballs) and *Kartoffelpuffer* (savoury potato pancakes) are Berlin specialities. However, young Germans are eschewing this diet and in an increasing number of restaurants the cuisine has been updated to reflect the taste for lighter fare.

KAISERSAAL (€€€)

This gourmet establishment serves superior à la carte cuisine, based on the classical German-French style. This is one of the top places to eat in Berlin and reservations are essential.
🔲 H6 ✉ Bellevuestrasse 1 (Sony Center), Potsdamer Platz ☎ 030 2575 14 54 🕐 Daily 7pm–midnight 🚇 S- and U-Bahn Potsdamer Platz

KAFKA (€)

Well-heeled twenty-some-things meet here for enticing meat and fish dishes, including Argentinian roast beef.
🔲 L7 ✉ Oranienstrasse 204 ☎ 030 612 24 29 🕐 Mon–Sat noon–1am, Sun 10am, Sun brunch 10–4 🚇 U-Bahn Görlitzer Banhof

KARTOFFEL KISTE (€€€)

Tuck into some wholesome and hearty German cooking at this cosy restaurant dedicated to the humble potato. Every dish contains potato in some shape or form, that even includes the pizza bases.
🔲 E6 ✉ Europa-Center 1, Etage ☎ 030 261 42 54 🕐 Daily 11.30am–midnight 🚇 S- and U-Bahn Zoologischer Garten

LUTTER & WEGNER (€€€)

This historic 19th-century restaurant on the Gendarmenmarkt has Austrian as well as German cuisine; also a wine bar.
🔲 J5 ✉ Charlottenstrasse 56 ☎ 030 20 29 54 10 🕐 Daily 11am–3am 🚇 U-Bahn Hausvogteiplatz-Stadtmitte

MARJELLCHEN (€€)

East Prussian cooking at good prices. Sorrel soup and Königsberg dumplings are specialities.
🔲 C7 ✉ Mommsenstrasse 9 ☎ 030 883 2676 🕐 Mon–Sat 5pm–midnight. Closed Sun in summer 🚇 S-Bahn Savignyplatz

RADKE'S GASTHAUS (€€€)

Attractive restaurant with old Berlin cooking.
🔲 E7 ✉ Marburger Strasse 16 ☎ 2134652 🕐 Mon–Sat noon–2am 🚇 U-Bahn Augsburger Strasse

STORCH (€€)

A jewel in the crown of Schöneberg restaurants. Volker Hauptvogel's virtuoso variations on Alsatian dishes are renowned; the tarte flambé is a local legend. No credit cards.
🔲 F8 ✉ Wartburgstrasse 54 ☎ 030 784 2059 🕐 Daily 6pm–1am 🚇 U-Bahn Eisenacher Strasse

VAU (€€€)

Currently one of the best restaurants in the city for its updated German-Austrian cuisine.
🔲 J5 ✉ Jägerstrasse 54–55 ☎ 030 20 97 30 🕐 Mon–Sat 12–2.30, 7–10.30 🚇 U-Bahn Französische Strasse

WEINSTEIN (€€)

This bistro is one of the best wine bars in the city, serving classic German and French food in tradtional surroundings.
🔲 L2 ✉ Lychener Strasse 33 ☎ 030 441 18 42 🕐 Mon–Sat 5pm–2am, Sun 6pm–2am 🚇 U-Bahn Eberswalder Strasse

Other European Restaurants

AUSTRIAN

DIENER (€€)
You are guaranteed to get a warm welcome at this cosy old-style Berlinpub serving top-notch Austrian Cuisine in Charlottenburg.
✚ D6 ✉ Grolmanstrasse 47 ☎ 030 881 53 29 ⏰ Daily 6pm–3am 🚇 S-Bahn Savignyplatz

SARAH WEINER (€€)
In a wing of the Hamburger Bahnhof (► 54), this is a great place to have a bite to eat after a morning of modern art appreciation. Enjoy some classic Austrian Cuisine in stylish contemporary surroundings.
✚ G4 ✉ Invalidenstrasse 50–51 ☎ 030 881 53 29 ⏰ Tue–Fri 10–6, Sat–Sun 11–6 🚇 S-Bahn Lehrter Bahnhof

FRENCH

ALT LUXEMBURG (€€€)
One of the best restaurants in the city. Chef Karl Wannemacher has a way with herbs.
✚ C6 ✉ Windscheidstrasse 31 ☎ 030 323 87 30 ⏰ Mon–Sat 5pm–midnight 🚇 U-Bahn Sophie-Charlotte-Platz

BORCHARDT (€€€)
A. F. W. Borchardt founded this top quality French restaurant in 1853. High ceiling, plush maroon benches, art nouveau mosaics and marble columns recreate 1920s café culture. Popular with politicians, actors and sports personalities, you may see a few stars at this well-known celebrity spot.
✚ J5 ✉ Französische Strasse 47 ☎ 030 20 38 71 10 ⏰ Daily 12–midnight 🚇 U-Bahn Französische Strasse

BOVRIL (€€€)
Bistro with fresh, beautifully presented, French-German food. Popular with businessmen and literati.
✚ E7 ✉ Ku'damm 184 ☎ 030 88184 61 ⏰ Mon–Sat 11am–1am 🚇 U-Bahn Uhlandstrasse

CAFÉ DE FRANCE (€€)
The food is traditionally French but the décor is modern at this popular bistro on Unter den Linden. Good price for great food.
✚ J5 ✉ Unter den Linden 62–68 ☎ 030 20 64 13 91 ⏰ Mon–Sat 10–10, Sun 10–6 🚇 S-Bahn Unter den Linden

GREEK

SKALES (€€)
The service is a little brusque, but the food is tasty and fresh at this modern Greek taverna in the heart of the city.
✚ K4 ✉ Rosenthaler Strasse 13 ☎ 030 283 30 06 ⏰ Daily 6pm–1am 🚇 U-Bahn Rosenthaler Platz

TAVERNA OUSIES (€€)
Be sure to reserve a table at this top-quality restaurant in Schöneberg —by far the best choice for classic Greek food in the city. Try the fresh sardines in lemon olive oil and the rich moussaka.
✚ F8 ✉ Grunewalderstrasse 16 ☎ 030 216 79 57 ⏰ Daily 5pm–late 🚇 U-Bahn Eisenacher Strasse

GERMAN WINES

Roman conquerors began growing wine in Germany more than 2,000 years ago. Today the country is divided into 13 distinct wine-growing regions, mainly along the Rhine and Moselle river valleys. Nearly all the wine is white, relying heavily on the Müller-Thurgau and Riesling grapes. Red wines are not generally held in high esteem and are not usually consumed locally. As a major wine producer, Germany offers a diverse range from earthy and dry to mellow and sweet. German wine laws require strict quality controls.

GOOD VALUE

Compared to other European capitals, Berlin is a relatively inexpensive place to eat out. Even a fantastic meal in a top-class restaurant is affordable when compared with the equivalent in Paris or London. Credit cards are not universally accepted though, so it is probably wise to carry cash with you.

ITALIAN

BOCCA DI BACCO (€€€)

This is the place to go for gourmet Italian food. The food is posh and the address exclusive, but the staff are friendly and welcoming. Reserve at night.

➕ J5 ✉ Friedrichstrasse 167–168 ☎ 030 20 67 28 28 🕐 Mon–Sat 12–midnight, Sun 6pm–midnight 🚇 S-Bahn Friedrichstrasse

CASOLARE (€)

The staff are vocal and entertaining, particularly during an Italian football final, at this bustling trattoria on a scenic corner in Kreuzberg. Come here for the best pizza in Berlin at the best prices. Reserve at night.

➕ L8 ✉ Grimmstrasse 30 ☎ 030 69 50 66 10 🕐 Daily noon–midnight 🚇 U- or S-Bahn Schönleinstrasse

OSSENA (€–€€)

The two branches of Ossena are bustling at any time of day, filled with visitors and locals alike who return again and again for the warm welcome and surroundings, prompt service and excellent Italian food at affordable prices. Their tiramisu is delicious and light.

➕ L7 ✉ Oranienstrasse 39 ☎ 030 615 26 22 🕐 6pm–midnight 🚇 U-Bahn Kottbusser Tor

Also at:

➕ K4 ✉ Rosenthaler Strasse 42 ☎ 030 280 998 77 🕐 6pm–midnight 🚇 S-Bahn Hackescher Markt

OXYMORON (€€)

Delicious Italian food is served at this 1920s style lounge in Hackesche Höfe. Enjoy a wonderful meal and then party into the night at their stylish bar with a dance floor.

➕ K4 ✉ Rosenthaler Strasse 40–41, Hackesche Höfe ☎ 030 28 39 18 86/28 39 18 88 🕐 Daily 11am–late, sunset club Wed 10am–midnight (Sep–Jun), Fri–Sat 11am–late 🚇 S-Bahn Hackescher Markt

DIE ZWÖLF APOSTEL (€–€€)

An ideal lunch or dinner spot for those visiting Museumsinsel (➤ 45). Red Velvet curtains, candlelight, painted ceilings and an open kitchen piled high with fresh ingredients all add to the theatrical experience. All pizzas are reduced between 12 and 4.

➕ J5 ✉ Georgenstrasse 2 ☎ 030 201 02 22 🕐 Daily 24 hours 🚇 S-Bahn Savignyplatz

MIXED EUROPEAN

BAMBERGER REITER (€€€)

Reservations are essential at this outstanding French/Italian restaurant.

➕ E7 ✉ Regensburgerstrasse 7 ☎ 030 21 96 63 55 🕐 Tue–Sat 6pm–1am 🚇 U-Bahn Spichernstrasse

GOURMETRESTAURANT LORENZ ADLON (€€€)

Sample some of the best gourmet fusion food in the city at this experimental restaurant in the exclusive and historic surroundings of the Hotel Adlon on Unter den Linden.

➕ J5 ✉ Unter den Linden 77 ☎ 030 226 10 🕐 Daily 7pm–midnight 🚇 S-Bahn Unter den Linden

FACIL (€€€)

This highly regarded Michelin starred restaurant in the Madison hotel serves Mediterranean gourmet cuisine with a French twist. Make sure you book a table at this popular Zen oasis in the heart of the city.
➕ H6 ✉ (In Hotel Madison), Potsdamer Strasse 3 ☎ 030 590 05 12 34 🕐 Mon–Fri 12–3, 7–11 🚇 S- or U-Bahn Potsdamer Platz

HUGOS (€€€)

The haute cuisine prepared by Chef Thomas Kammeler has been awarded 1 Michelin star—one of only a few restaurants in the city to receive the accolade. Worth it for the splendid panoramic views over Berlin from the roof.
➕ F6 ✉ (In Hotel Inter-Continental), Budapester Strasse ☎ 030 26 02 12 63 🕐 Mon–Sat 6pm–10.30 🚇 S- and U-Bahn Zoologischer Garten

MARE BÊ (€€)

Reservations are essential at this outstanding French/Italian restaurant.
➕ K4 ✉ Rosenthaler Strasse 46-48 ☎ 030 28 36 545 🕐 Mon–Thu 12–midnight, Fri 6pm–1am, Sat–Sun 6pm–late 🚇 S-Bahn Hackescher Markt

MARGAUX (€€€)

Expect a few avant-garde creations and some classic à la carte dishes at this 1 Michelin star first-rate restaurant on Unter den Linden
➕ J5 ✉ Unter den Linden 78 ☎ 030 22 65 26 11 🕐 Tue–Sat 12–2, 7–10.30 🚇 S-Bahn Unter den Linden

PORTUGUESE

CARAVELA (€)

Wonderful grilled fish in a southern suburb.
➕ Off map ✉ Dickhardstrasse 27 ☎ 030 852 26 60 🕐 Daily 5pm–midnight 🚇 U-Bahn Walther-Schreiber-Platz

RUSSIAN

PASTERNAK (€)

Marina Lehmann's lovely restaurant has a literary theme. Book ahead.
➕ L3 ✉ Knaackstrasse 24 ☎ 030 441 33 99 🕐 Daily noon–2am 🚇 U-Bahn Senefelderplatz

SPANISH

LA PALOMA (€€)

Bright and airy spot for paella, sangria and other Iberian fare.
➕ M7 ✉ Skalitzerstrasse 54 ☎ 030 61 28 73 43 🕐 Daily 5pm–1am 🚇 U-Bahn Görlitzer Bahnhof

MAR Y SOL (€)

Come here for some of the tastiest and fastest tapas in the city. The food is authentic and the crowd is load. Reserve in advance.
➕ D6 ✉ Savignyplatz 5 ☎ 030 313 25 93 🕐 Daily 11.30am–late 🚇 S-Bahn Savignyplatz

MUYFÁCIL (€)

This Spanish restaurant is great value for money. Their extensive cocktail and wine menu rivals any found in a gourmet restaurant and the fish and lobster dishes are fantastic.
➕ K4 ✉ Gormannstrasse 22 ☎ 030 28 59 90 26 🕐 Daily 10am–2am 🚇 U-Bahn Weinmeisterstrasse

---

AT THE WÜRSTCHENBUDE

Sausage stands (*Würstchenbudes*) and snack bars (*Schnellimbiss*) are popular in Germany with people who want to have a quick bite to eat on the run. These stands usually offer *Thüringer Bratwurst* (grilled sausage), the spicier *Krakauer* and *Frankfurter Bockwurst*. These are normally served in a bread roll with mustard. Bigger stands offer a choice of french fries, potato salad and *sauerkraut* (pickled cabbage). Other snacks include hamburger meat balls, served hot or cold. These are called *Buletten* in Berlin or *Frikadellen* elsewhere.

International Restaurants

HEALTH ON THE MENU

Recent food scares in Germany and abroad may prompt health-conscious Germans to change their eating habits. Traditionally veal and pork have been part of their staple diet but poultry, fish and non-meat dishes are gaining popularity both at home and in restaurants. The numbers of Oriental and vegetarian establishments have been climbing as well.

AMERICAN

THE SIXTIES (€€)

This is the best place in the city to grab a burger and fries or a hearty steak and sample the retro American diner experience.
✚ J4 ✉ Oranienburger Strasse 11 ☎ 030 28 59 90 41 🕐 Sun–Thu 10am–2am, Fri–Sat 10am–4am 🚇 S-Bahn Hackescher Markt

CHINESE

AROMA (€€)

If it's dim sum you're after this is the place to go. The furnishings may be a little dated, but the Cantonese dishes are first class.
✚ C6 ✉ Kantstrasse 35 ☎ 030 37 59 16 28 🕐 Daily noon–3am 🚇 U-Bahn Wilmersdorfer Strasse

INDIAN

AMRIT (€€)

The warm surroundings, friendly, attentive staff, excellent food and fruity cocktails make this Indian restaurant a popular choice for locals and visitors alike.
✚ L7 ✉ Oranienstrasse 202–203 ☎ 030 612 55 50 🕐 Sun–Thu noon–1am, Fri and Sat noon–2am 🚇 U-Bahn Görlitzer Bahnhof
Also at:
✚ J4 ✉ Oranienburger Strasse 45 ☎ 030 28 88 48 40 🕐 Sun–Thu noon–1am, Fri, Sat noon–2am 🚇 S-Bahn Oranienburger Strasse

YOGI SNACK (€€)

Reservations are essential on the weekends at this popular little Indian restaurant off the beaten track. The food is fabulous and the price tag is certainly reasonable for the quality food.
✚ Off map ✉ Simon-Dach-Strasse 11 ☎ 030 29004838 🕐 Daily noon–late 🚇 U-Bahn Frankenfurter Tor

INDONESIAN

MIRCHI (€€)

Good food is guaranteed at this Indian and Singaporean fusion restaurant and cocktail bar in Mitte. The daily lunch menu has a good range of vegetarian, chicken and lamb dishes at an affordable price.
✚ J4 ✉ Oranienburger Strasse 50 ☎ 030 28 44 44 82 🕐 Daily noon–1am 🚇 U-Bahn Oranienburger Tor

JAPANESE

SHABU–JO (€€)

The main attraction here is the Japanese fondue, which is great to share and provides excellent value for money.
✚ J6 ✉ Kronenstrasse 55–56 ☎ 030 22 48 77 01 🕐 Mon–Fri noon–1am, Sat–Sun 1pm–1am 🚇 U-Bahn Stadtmitte

SUMO (€)

This modern, stylish sushi bar in Kreuzberg has an excellent choice of expertly prepared raw fish and a great selection of Japanese beers and green teas.
✚ J8 ✉ Bergmannstrasse 89 ☎ 030 69 00 49 63 🕐 Daily noon–midnight 🚇 U-Bahn Gneisenaustrasse

KOREAN

KWANG JU GRILL (€)

The South Korean chef serves up huge portions of sweet and sour chicken, pork ribs and more.

🚻 D8 ✉ Emser Strasse 24 ☎ 030 883 97 94 🕐 Daily noon–midnight 🚇 U-Bahn Hohenzollernplatz

THAI

MAO THAI (€€)

An intimate cellar restaurant. Try the pineapple and coconut filled with shrimp.

🚻 L3 ✉ Wörther Strasse 30 ☎ 030 441 92 61 🕐 Daily noon–midnight 🚇 U-Bahn Senefelderplatz

PAPAYA (€€)

Come here for gourmet Thai food at affordable prices. The soups are very filling and the spicy stews are delicious. Make sure you book a table at the weekends, particularly if you want a table outside in the summer.

🚻 Off map ✉ Krossener Strasse 11 ☎ 030 29 77 12 31 🕐 Daily noon–midnight 🚇 S- and U-Bahn Warschauer Strasse

VEGETARIAN

HAKUIN (€€)

Hakuin has a reputation for being the best vegetarian restaurant in Berlin. European, Indian, Asian and Latin American dishes are lovingly prepared.

🚻 F7 ✉ Martin-Luther-Strasse 1/1a ☎ 030 218 20 27 🕐 Tue–Sat 5pm–11.30, Sun noon–11.30 🚇 U-Bahn Wittenbergplatz

SOPHIES WELTEN (€)

Enjoy wholesome vegetarian cooking at low prices at this bright, funky restaurant in Prenzlauer Berg.

🚻 L2 ✉ Dunckerstrasse 2a ☎ 030 54 71 34 77 🕐 Daily 5pm–midnight 🚇 U-Bahn Eberswalder Strasse

MIDDLE EASTERN

BAGDAD (€€)

One of Kreuzberg's most popular haunts. The garden is a plus for summer dining. Belly dancing on weekends.

🚻 N7 ✉ Schlesische Strasse 2 ☎ 030 612 69 62 🕐 Daily noon–1am 🚇 U-Bahn Schlesisches Tor

SUFISSIMO (€)

Freshly prepared couscous based dishes on the menu at this café and Persian restaurant in Kreuzberg.

🚻 K8 ✉ Fichtstrasse 1 ☎ 030 61 62 08 33 🕐 Daily 4pm–late 🚇 U-Bahn Südstern

TURKISH

HIT IT (€€)

Traditional spicy meat and vegetarian dishes are carefully prepared by an inventive chef.

🚻 B5 ✉ Knobelsdorffstrasse 35 ☎ 030 322 45 57 🕐 Mon–Thu 5pm–midnight, Sun 11am–midnight 🚇 U-Bahn Sophie-Charlotte-Platz

ISTANBUL (€€)

This well-known establishment is not cheap but the food is authentic.

🚻 D7 ✉ Pestalozzistrasse 84 ☎ 030 883 27 77 🕐 Daily noon–midnight 🚇 S-Bahn Savignyplatz

LITTLE ISTANBUL

Kreuzberg, a traditional working-class district near the centre of Berlin, has the largest Turkish community outside Istanbul. In the exotic neighbourhoods of Kottbusser Tor and Schlesisches Tor dozens of restaurants offer inexpensive and authentic Anatolian cuisine.

Cafés

ANYONE FOR COFFEE?

Café culture continues to thrive in the capital. Sunday brunch is a traditional weekend pastime among Berliners and afternoon *kafee* and *kuchen* (coffee and cake) is still standard practice. Traditional and independent cafés are thriving, but the American-style coffee chains are beginning to make their presence felt.

VEGETARIAN CAFÉ

Café Oren (€) is a light and airy café-restaurant near the Synagogue. An exotic mix of Israeli and Middle Eastern dishes; red wine from the Golan Heights.
✚ J4 ✉ Oranienburger Strasse 28 ☎ 030 282 82 28 🕐 Daily noon–midnight 🚇 S-Bahn Hackescher Markt

BARCOMI'S DELI (€)

Friendly courtyard deli with an enticing range of American snacks—everything from bagels to chocolate cake.
✚ K4 ✉ Bergamnnstrasse 21 ☎ 030 694 81 38 🕐 Mon–Sat 9am–10pm, Sun 10–10 🚇 U-Bahn Mehringdamm

CAFÉ AEDES-WEST (€€)

A trendy spot for those who want to see and be seen. There is an art gallery too.
✚ D6 ✉ Savignyplatz ☎ 030 312 55 04 🕐 Mon–Fri 8am–midnight, Sat, Sun 9am–midnight 🚇 S-Bahn Savignyplatz

CAFÉ BRAVO (€€)

The two cube-shaped areas with mirrored walls and transparent ceilings, designed by the American artist Dan Graham, form an unusual and contemporary meeting and eating space at the heart of the Kunstwerke Institute.
✚ J4 ✉ Auguststrasse 69, in der Kunstwerke ☎ 01 79 113 85 57 🕐 Daily 11am–midnight 🚇 U-Bahn Oranienburger Tor

CAFÉ EINSTEIN (€€)

Traditional Viennese-style coffee house trying to re-create a pre-war Berlin café atmosphere. There are newspapers and a garden, but prices are steep.
✚ F7 ✉ Kurfürstenstrasse 58 ☎ 030 204 36 32 🕐 Daily10am–2am 🚇 U-Bahn Nollendorfplatz

CAFÉ GELATO (€)

Eat in or takeaway at this café and ice-cream parlour on the top floor of the Potsdamer Platz Arkaden. They have the most extensive selection of ice-cream and sorbet in the city; how about maracuja, pocket coffee or old favourite chocolate?
✚ H6 ✉ Potsdamer Platz Arkaden Einkauf-Center ☎ 030 25 29 78 32 🕐 Mon–Thu and Sun 10am–11pm, Fri–Sat 10am–midnight 🚇 S- and U-Bahn Potsdamer Platz

CAFÉ IM LITERATURHAUS WINTERGARTEN (€€)

On the ground floor of a beautiful 19th-century villa, this traditional coffee house is certainly one of Berlin's most popular Sunday brunch venues. Waiters in dinner jackets and bow ties are keen to introduce you to the delights of the extensive cake buffet and you can sit out in the wonderful garden during the summer.
✚ E7 ✉ Fasanenstrasse 23 ☎ 030 882 54 14 🕐 Daily 9.30am–1am 🚇 U-Bahn Kurfürstendamm

CAFÉ LAPIS LAZULI (€)

This café in an 18th-century restored house serves lots of international fusion dishes and vegetarian options with breakfast till 3pm. Regular live music.
✚ Off map ✉ Benkerstrasse 21 ☎ 0331 280 23 71 🕐 Daily 10am–1am 🚇 S-Bahn Potsdam Stadt

CAFÉ M (€€)

One of Schöneberg's most popular late-night haunts, with non-stop breakfasts. No frills, but you'll get lots of atmosphere.

F8 ✉ Goltzstrasse 33
☎ 030 216 70 90 🕐 Daily
9am–1am 🚇 U-Bahn
Eisenacherstrasse

CAFÉ ÜBERSEE (€)

Busy into the early hours,
this attractive Kreuzberg
café on the canal bank
serves breakfast until 4pm
daily.

L7 ✉ Paul-Lincke-Ufer 44
☎ 030 618 87 65 🕐 Daily
10am–2am 🚇 U-Bahn
Kottbusser Tor

CAFÉ AM UFER (€)

This garden café is a great
place to be when the
weather is warm. Bask in
the sunshine on the
terrace over a coffee or ice
tea or enjoy breakfast,
lunch or a light evening
meal outside.

L7 ✉ Paul-Lincke-Ufer 42
☎ 030 61 62 92 00 🕐 Daily
10am–late 🚇 U-Bahn Paul-
Lincke-Ufer, Kottbusser Tor,
Schönleinstrasse

DAILY COFFEE (€)

A great way to kick-start
your day is to try the
American way at this
bagel and coffee house
that opens every day early
till late.

H6 ✉ Friedrich-Ebert-
Strase 31 🕐 Daily 9am–late
🚇 S-Bahn Potsdam Stadt

**OPERNPALAIS UNTER
LINDEN (€)**

Redolent of old Berlin,
this palatial café with
an expensive restaurant
upstairs is next to
the Staatsoper.

J5 ✉ Unter den Linden 5
☎ 030 20 26 83 🕐 Daily
8am–midnight 🚇 U-Bahn
Französische Strasse

SCHWARZES CAFÉ (€€)

Nightclubbers on their way
home meet businesspeople
setting off for work.

D6 ✉ Kantstrasse 148
☎ 030 313 80 38
🕐 Wed–Mon 24 hours, Tue
noon–3am 🚇 S-Bahn
Savignyplatz

SOUP-KULTUR (€)

The last word in snacks
plus a selection of the
world's tastiest soups.

D7 ✉ Kurfürstendamm
224 ☎ 030 88 62 92 82
🕐 Mon–Fri noon–7pm, Sat
noon–6pm 🚇 U-Bahn
Kurfürstendamm

**TADSCHIKISCHE
TEESTUBE (€€)**

A strictly no-smoking tea
house where footsore
visitors to the Mitte can
kick off their shoes and
loll on Tadzhik divans.

J5 ✉ Am Festungsgraben 1
☎ 030 201 06 93 🕐 Mon–Fri
5pm–midnight, Sat–Sun
3pm–midnight 🚇 S-Bahn
Friedrichstrasse

**TIM'S CANADIAN
DELI (€)**

Busy café convenient to
the weekend market on
Winterfeldtplatz.
Brownies and muffins.

F7 ✉ Maassenstrasse 14
☎ 030 21 75 69 60
🕐 Mon–Thu 8am–1am, Fri, Sat
3pm–1am, Sun 9am–1am
🚇 U-Bahn Nollendorfplatz

ZUM NUSSBAUM (€)

A traditional Berlin
Gasthaus located near
Fischerinsel in
Nikolaiviertel.

K5 ✉ Am Nussbaum 3
☎ 030 242 30 95 🕐 Daily
noon–3am 🚇 U-Bahn
Klosterstrasse

BREAKFAST IN BERLIN

For Berliners, breakfast is a
way of life. You can, it seems,
take the meal at any time of
the day, and you can spend
as long over it as you like.
Ham and eggs, sausage,
cheese, muesli, pumpernickel
and even cakes may be on
the agenda.

Department Stores & Souvenirs

SHOPPING HOURS

Most shops open between 9 and 10am and close at 6 or 6.30pm. Many are closed on Saturday afternoon.

APPELMANN GALERIE SHOP

There is a huge variety of souvenirs bearing the green and red 'Ampelmann' logo in this shop dedicated to the cult hat-wearing celebrity from Berlin's pedestrian crossings.
✚ K4 ✉ Hackesche Höfe Hof V ☎ 030 44 04 88 09 🕐 Mon–Sat 10–8, Sun 11–7 Ⓢ S-Bahn Hackescher Markt

FACHHANDELSGWSCH ÄFT RASCHKE

If you miss out on Berlin's Christmas markets, you can still find traditional wooden, handmade Christmas decorations here.
✚ K4 ✉ Neuer Hackescher Markt, Dircksenstrasse 50 ☎ 030 28 38 80 10 Ⓢ S-Bahn Hackescher Markt

GALERIES LAFAYETTE

Branch of the Parisian shopping mecca. An architectural treat too, with its impressive curved glass wall, curved roof and two huge glass cones inside.
✚ J5 ✉ Französischestrasse 76–78 ☎ 030 20 94 80 🕐 Mon–Fri 9.30am–8pm, Sat 9am–4pm Ⓢ U-Bahn Französische Strasse

KADEWE (KAUFHAUS DES WESTENS)

The second largest department store in the world (after Harrods of London), stocking some 250,000 items. The wonderful Food Hall is a must (► 77).
✚ F7 ✉ Tauentzienstrasse 21–24 ☎ 030 212 10 🕐 Mon–Fri 9.30–8, Sat 9–4 Ⓢ U-Bahn Wittenbergplatz

KAUFHAUS KREUZBERG

This unconventional shopping arcade in Kreuzberg has 50 shops catering for alternative shoppers.
✚ L7 ✉ Adalbertstrasse 97 am Kottbusser Tor ☎ 030 61 65 96 12 🕐 Mon–Sat 12–8 Ⓢ U-Bahn Kottbusser Tor, Görlitzer Bahnhof

KAUFHOF

This western department store occupies the premises of an outmoded East German predecessor.
✚ L4 ✉ Alexanderplatz ☎ 030 24 74 30 🕐 Daily 9–8 Ⓢ U- or S-Bahn Alexanderplatz

NATURKAUFHAUS

On the attractive shopping street of Schlossstrasse there are 7 floors of eco-friendly fashion, jewellery, household items, stationery and cosmetics.
✚ Off map ✉ Galleria Schlossstrasse ☎ 030 797 37 16 🕐 Mon–Fri 10–8, Sat 10–6 Ⓢ U-Bahn Schlossstrasse, Rathaus Steglitz

POTSDAMER PLATZ ARKADEN

The architecturally noteworthy Renzo Piano mall has 120 shops, plus cafés and restaurants.
✚ H6 ✉ Potsdamer Platz Ⓢ U- or S-Bahn Potsdamer Platz

POST–KARTEN

Huge range of postcards and cards that come as a refreshing alternative to those found in tourist shop and kiosks.
✚ J4 ✉ Oranienburger Strasse 51 ☎ 030 28 09 62 30 Ⓢ U-Bahn Oranienburger Tor, S-Bahn Oranienburger Strasse

Boutiques & Designer Clothes

BAGAGE

This Kreuzberg shop sells bags of all shapes, sizes and colours—everything from handbags and satchels to rucksacks and travel bags.

✚ J8 ✉ Bergmannstrasse 13 ☎ 030 693 89 16 🚇 U-Bahn Gneisenaustrasse

BERGMANN

This friendly boutique brings all the latest men's and women's fashion labels together under one roof including Diesel, Energie Firetrap, Miss Sixty, Ana Alcazar, Freesoul and Custo Barcelona.

✚ J8 ✉ Bergmannstrasse 2 ☎ 030 694 03 90 🚇 U-Bahn Mehringdamm

DIESEL

A large shop selling the latest lines from this well-known international brand.

✚ E7 ✉ Kurfürstendamm 17 ☎ 030 88 55 14 55 🚇 U-Bahn Kurfürstendamm

EISDIELER

A showcase for young Berlin designers.

✚ J4 ✉ Kastanienallee 12 ☎ 030 285 73 51 🚇 U-Bahn Oranienburger Tor

ENERGIE STORE

Stylish retro casual wear, jeans and accessories for men and women.

✚ E7 ✉ Tautentzienstrasse 15 ☎ 030 23 60 99 40 🚇 U-Bahn Kurfürstendamm

G-STAR STORE

There is an excellent choice of stylish designer denim for men and women at this Dutch store in the heart of the city.

✚ E7 ✉ Oranienburger Strasse ☎ 030 24 63 25 54 🚇 S-Bahn Hackescher Markt

HOGI'S

A little shop in Prenzlauer Berg that stocks a great selection of women's fashion labels such as Morgan, Muchacha, Freesoul and Ana Alcazar.

✚ C3 ✉ Rykestrasse 11 ☎ 030 44 04 22 28 🚇 U-Bahn Eberswalderstrasse

JIL SANDER

Here you get understated but eye-catching fashions from the celebrity German designer.

✚ D7 ✉ Kurfürstendamm 185 ☎ 030 886 70 20 🚇 U-Bahn Uhlandstrasse

JIMMY'S

Designer retro sports gear and jeans for trendy casual girls and boys.

✚ J4 ✉ Oranienburger Strasse 8 ☎ 030 27 59 48 30 🚇 S-Bahn Hackescher Markt

NIX MODE-DESIGN

Chic clothing for men, women and children. The shop is located in Mitte.

✚ J4 ✉ Oranienburger Strasse 32, in den Heckmann Höfen ☎ 030 281 80 44 🚇 U-Bahn Oranienburger Tor

STOFFWECHSEL

This friendly shop stocks a vast array of funky and fashionable labels such as Miss Sixty, Firetrap, Only, G-Star and Energie. All you will need to look your best and feel at home in Berlin's bars and clubs.

✚ K4 ✉ Alte Schönhauser Strasse 20–22 ☎ 030 28 87 96 33 🚇 U-Bahn Weinmeister Strasse

CITY ORIGINALS

Where fashion is concerned, Berlin is not a city you would mention in the same breath as Paris, London, or Milan, but Berliners are as style-conscious as the inhabitants of any other cosmopolitan city. The boutiques off the Ku'damm—for example in Knesebeckstrasse, Uhlandstrasse or Pariserstrasse—include some of the city's own fashion houses, promoting the creations of Patrick Hellmann, Jutta Meierling and others.

Second-hand & Offbeat

THE ALTERNATIVE SCENE

Berlin's chic cosmopolitan image is constantly being undermined by a brazenly nonconformist alternative with roots in the 1960s. There is plenty of evidence of the latter in the remarkable variety of stores specializing in second-hand and offbeat clothing and jewellery. You can have great fun inspecting the wares. A good starting point is the Garage, which sells used clothes by the kilo. The more discerning should head for Kastanienallee.

COLOURS

Delve through original clothing from 1950s to the 1990s and furniture from the 1960s and 1970s in over 1,000sq m (10,750sq ft) of floor space.

✚ J8 ✉ Bergmannstrasse 102 ☎ 030 694 33 48 Ⓤ U-Bahn Mehringdamm

DIE KAKTUSBLÜTE

This shop will style you from head to toe in designer clothing and accessories from the 1960s and 1970s. They also do retro hair and makeup.

✚ K2 ✉ Schönhauser Allee 52a ☎ J01 73 832 12 00 Ⓤ U-Bahn Eberswalder Strasse

FRANZ & JOSEPH SCHEIBEN

The friendly staff will be glad to help you rifle through the racks of rare vinyl and second-hand CDs.

✚ K3 ✉ Kastanienalle 48 ☎ 030 41 71 46 82 Ⓤ U-Bahn Rosenthaler Platz

GARAGE

Clothes are sold by weight in this large warehouse near Nollendorfplatz U-Bahn station. It claims to be Europe's biggest second-hand store.

✚ F7 ✉ Ahornstrasse 2 ☎ 030 211 27 60 Ⓤ U-Bahn Nollendorfplatz

KAUFHAUS SCHRILL

Showy accessories—everything from hats and gloves to ties and loud jewellery. The roll-call of former patrons is said to include Sylvester Stallone.

✚ D6 ✉ Bleibtreustrasse 46 ☎ 030 882 40 48 Ⓢ S-Bahn Savignyplatz

KNOPF-PAUL

The ingenious owner of this Kreuzberg shop makes buttons out of everything—even plum stones and typewriter keys.

✚ J8 ✉ Zossener Strasse 10 ☎ 030 692 12 12 Ⓤ U-Bahn Gneisenaustrasse

MADE IN BERLIN

Second-hand clothes of quality, including 1920s cocktail dresses and tuxedos from the 1950s. Also plenty of antique Levis, hippy clothing, leather jackets and 1970s shirts—all you will need for an authentic retro look.

✚ G8 ✉ Potsdamer Strasse 105 ☎ 030 262 24 31 Ⓤ U-Bahn Kurfürstenstrasse

SERGEANT PEPPERS

In the funky shopping street of Kastanienallee, Sergeant Peppers is the place to shop for authentic 1960s clothing. They have an excellent selection of original antique clothing for men and women including bathing suits and bikinis.

✚ K3 ✉ Kastanienallee 91–92 ☎ 030 448 11 21 Ⓤ U-Bahn Eberswalder Strasse, Senefelder Strasse

STERLING GOLD

This shop in Mitte has an impressive range of glamorous evening, ball and cocktail wear from the 1950s to the 1980s. An added bonus is that the shop has its own dressmaker who can transform any dress into a perfect fit.

✚ J4 ✉ Oranienburger Strasse 105 ☎ 030 28 09 65 00 Ⓢ S-Bahn Hackescher Markt

Galleries

ARNDT AND PARTNER

A stimulating collection of experimental art in Mitte, including works by internationally renowned artists and local stars.

✚ K4 ✉ Auguststrasse 35
☎ 030 280 81 23 🕓 Tue–Sat
2pm–7pm 🚇 U-Bahn
Rosenthaler Platz

ASIAN FINE ARTS

This gallery exhibits modern Chinese, Japanese, Korean and Indonesian works of art and the managers go to great lengths to promote Asian arts and increase its profile.

✚ K4 ✉ 1st Hof,
Sophienstrasse 18 ☎ 030
28391387 🕓 Tue–Sat
noon–7pm 🚇 U-Bahn
Weinmeisterstrasse

DAAD

Avant-garde and modern art.

✚ F5 ✉ Kurfürstenstrasse 58
☎ 030 261 36 40 🕓 Daily
12.30–7 🚇 U-Bahn
Nollendorfplatz 🚌 Bus 100

EIGEN AND ART

Experimental art is on display at this rustic gallery in Mitte. Most of the works exhibited are by artists from the former East Germany.

✚ J4 ✉ Auguststrasse 26
☎ 030 280 66 05 🕓 Tue–Fri
2pm–7pm; Sat 11am–5pm
🚇 S-Bahn Oranienburger Tor

GALERIE BRUSBERG

The place to come for Dada and surrealist art, plus the occasional Picasso and Miró.

✚ E7 ✉ Ku'damm 213
☎ 030 881 81 61 🕓 Tue–Fri
10–6.30, Sat 10–2 🚇 U-Bahn
Uhlandstrasse

GALERIE PELS-LEUSDEN

International art of the 19th and 20th centuries, displayed in the beautiful former home of turn-of-the-20th-century architect Hans Grisebach.

✚ E7 ✉ Fasanenstrasse 25
☎ 030 885 91 50
🕓 Mon–Fri 10–6.30, Sat 10–2
🚇 U-Bahn Uhlandstrasse

GALERIE WOHNMASCHINE

Promotes the work of up-and-coming but impoverished artists.

✚ J4 ✉ Tucholskystrasse 34
☎ 030 30 87 20 15
🕓 Tue–Fri 2–7, Sat noon–5
🚇 S-Bahn Oranienburger
Strasse

HACKESCHE HÖFE

Now smartened up and commericalized, these historic courtyards remain at the heart of Berlin's contemporary art scene with their galleries, workshops and cafés.

✚ K4 ✉ Rosenthaler Strasse
40–41 ☎ No phone
🚇 S-Bahn Hackescher Markt

KUNST-WERKE BERLIN

Experimental and avant-garde art in one of Auguststrasse's new galleries.

✚ J4 ✉ Auguststrasse 69
☎ 030 243 45 90 🚇 S-Bahn
Oranienburger Strasse

TACHELES

Splendidly dilapidated this former squat remains a centre of experimental and offbeat art. Watch resident artists at work.

✚ J4 ✉ Oranienburger Strasse
53 ☎ 030 282 61 85
🚇 S-Bahn Oranienburger Strasse

ART OF ALL KINDS

Artists generally divide into two groups: the up-and-coming and those who have already made it. The exclusive private galleries around Fasanenstrasse promote the work of established German artists while also exhibiting some of the best in international modern art. The other side of the coin is the collection of crumbling ateliers and studios in Kreuzberg and the Scheunenviertel, where the undiscovered, neglected and uncompromising show off their work.

Home Furnishings & Accessories

ROYAL PORCELAIN

Berlin's historic association with porcelain dates from 1763 when Frederick the Great founded the Königliche Porzellan Manufaktor (Royal Porcelain Factory, or KPM). It is still going strong today. The firm's principal outlet (with showroom) is on the Ku'damm, but the famous KPM hallmark crops up all over the city. The best place to see the historic pieces is the Belvedere at Schloss Charlottenburg (➤ 33).

ART & INDUSTRY

Furniture, lamps and accessories in Bauhaus and other functionalist styles. They also sell watches.

🚇 D7 ✉ Bleibtreustrasse 40
☎ 030 883 39 42 🚉 S-Bahn Savignyplatz

BELLA CASA

Affordable and attractive ethnic furnishings from North Africa and Egypt.

🚇 J8 ✉ Bergmannstrasse 101 ☎ 030 694 0784
🚉 U-Bahn Mehringdamm

DADRIADE

A flagship store in Mitte that attracts Italian style seekers.

🚇 K4 ✉ Rosenthaler Strasse 40–41 ☎ 030 2852 8720
🚉 S-Bahn Hackescher Markt

DOM

This shiny shop near Hackescher Markt is the place to go to inject some glitz and glamour into your life. Add a touch of sparkle to your home with their kitsch accessories and lamps or treat a friend to one of their innovative gifts.

🚇 J5 ✉ Friedrichstrasse 76
☎ 030 20 94 73 95
🚉 S-Bahn Friedrcihstrasse
Also at:
🚇 K4 ✉ Hackescher Markt
☎ 030 28 09 83 67
🚉 S-Bahn Hackescher Markt

GURU-LADEN

Everything you need to give your home an exotic facelift. Yards of printed textiles, bright, patterned ceramics, Buddhas, sculptural lamps, chunky furniture, banana leaf notebooks and recycled paper products from India, Nepal, Mexico and Africa.

🚇 L2 ✉ Pappelallee 2
☎ 030 44 01 33 72 🚉 U-Bahn Eberswalder Strasse

KPM

Quality porcelain bearing the renowned KPM hallmark (see panel).

🚇 C7 ✉ Kurfürstendamm 27
☎ 030 386 72 10 🚉 U-Bahn Adenauerplatz

MEISSENER PORZELLAN

Figurines and other decorative items made of Meissen porcelain.

🚇 D7 ✉ Kurfürstendamm 26a ☎ 030 88 68 35 30
🚉 U-Bahn Uhlandstrasse
Also at:
🚇 J5 ✉ Unter den Linden 39B
☎ 030 22 67 90 28
🚉 S-Unter den Linden

RUBY

A small minimalist shop in a restored courtyard selling top-of-the-range designer furniture, ceramics, lamps, rugs, fabrics and candles.

🚇 J4 ✉ Oranienburger Strasse 32 ☎ 030 28 38 60 30
🚉 S-Bahn Oranienburger Strasse

RUSSISCHE SAMOWARE

Beautiful antique Russian samovars dating back to before the Revolution.

🚇 E7 ✉ Marburger Strasse 5
☎ 030 211 36 66 🚉 U-Bahn Augsburger Strasse

SEIDEL UND SOHN

This antique shop specializes in Biedermeier furniture and household items.

🚇 F8 ✉ Eisenacher Strasse 113 ☎ 030 216 18 50
🚉 U-Bahn Eisenacher Strasse

Markets & Food Shops

ANTIK UND FLOHMARKT

Affordable antiques and bric-à-brac beneath the arches of Friedrichstrasse station.

⊞ J5 ⊠ Georgenstrasse
☎ 030 208 26 45
🕓 Wed–Mon 11–6 🚇 U- or S-Bahn Friedrichstrasse

BERLINER KUNST-UND-NOSTALGIE-MARKT

Art and nostalgia—for the most part paintings, drawings and antiques.

⊞ J5 ⊠ Am Kupfergraben
🚇 U- or S-Bahn Friedrichstrasse

FASSBENDER AND RAUSCH

Founded by Heinrich Fassbender and Wilhelm Rausch in the 19th century, this luxury chocolate shop and confectioner is always busy.

⊞ J5 ⊠ Charlottenstrasse 60
☎ 030 20 45 84 40
🚇 U-Bahn Stadtmitte

GALERIES LAFAYETTE FOOD HALL

Berliners flock to the delicatessen in the basement. Sip champagne, sample exquisite pastries and track down some of the smelliest French cheese in the city.

⊠ Basement, Galeries Lafayette (► 72)

KADEWE FOOD HALL

Europe's largest delicatessen. Food and drink from around the world: lobster and caviar, exotic vegetables and spices—and over 1,000 varieties of German sausage.

⊠ Sixth floor, KaDeWe (► 72)

KÖNIGSBERGER MARZIPAN

This long-running, family confectioners in Charlottenburg is the place to go to sample some traditional German marzipan. Their boxes of assorted sweets make great gifts to take home.

⊞ C6 ⊠ Pestalozzistrasse 54a
☎ 030 323 82 54 🚇 U-Bahn Sophie-Charlotte-Platz

STRASSE DES 17. JUNI

This is one of the largest flea markets in Berlin, popular with tourists who like to rummage for a retro bargain or hunt down rare antiques.

⊞ E5 ⊠ Tiergarten ☎ 030 26 55 00 96 🕓 Sat, Sun 10–5
🚇 S-Bahn Tiergarten

TRÖDELMARKT AM RATHAUS SCHÖNEBERG

A market in the Tiergarten, popular with antiques dealers and tourists.

⊞ E5 ⊠ John-F.-Kennedy Platz 🕓 Sat, Sun 9–4
🚇 S-Bahn Tiergarten

TÜRKISCHER MARKT

An intriguing market in the heart of the Turkish community, offering choice ethnic food including olives, cheeses and spiced chicken.

⊞ L8 ⊠ Maybachufer
🕓 Tue–Fri noon–6.30
🚇 U-Bahn Schönleinstrasse

WINTERFELDTMARKT

A favourite with Berliners, this Schöneberg market is one of the city's liveliest. Have brunch in one of the local cafés.

⊞ F7 ⊠ Winterfeldtplatz
🕓 Wed and Sat 8–1
🚇 U-Bahn Nollendorfplatz

WINTERFELDTPLATZ

One pleasant way to while away a Saturday morning is to explore the antiques shops around Motzstrasse, before homing in on one of Berlin's most colourful and entertaining street markets, in Winterfeldtplatz. You never know quite what you will find here, which is the main attraction—everything from hand-me-down jewellery to books with faded covers, from flowers to children's clothes. Having worked up an appetite, visit one of the numerous cafés serving breakfast in the vicinity–try Tim's Canadian Deli on Maassenstrasse (► 71).

The Best of the Rest

FRIEDRICHSTRASSE

Rebuilt almost from scratch during the last decade, Friedrichstrasse is rapidly becoming a magnet for discerning shoppers, especially aficionados of the latest designer fashions. Galeries Lafayette (► 72), also here, is the first branch of the famous department store outside France. Apart from Jean Nouvel's highly innovative open-plan design, the main talking point is the mouth-watering Food Hall, selling everything from pâtés to oysters.

EUROPA-CENTER

There are more than 100 shops in the high-rise shopping mall known as the Europa Center. Take a lift to the viewing platform on the 22nd floor for unbeatable views of Berlin.

AUSTRALIA SHOPPING WORLD

This Aussie shop stocks a wide selection of antipodean wines, beers and spirits. There is also an extensive range of travel guidebooks to choose from and novels with an Australian accent.
- ➕ K6 ✉ Wallstrasse 66
- ☎ 0221 12 16 17
- 🚇 U-Bahn Märkisches Museum

BELLADONNA

This shop in Kreuzberg has an impressive range of natural and aromatherapy cosmetics from German companies such as Logona, Lavera, Dr. Hauschka and Weleda, as well as essential oils from Primavera.
- ➕ J8 ✉ Bergmannstrasse 101
- ☎ 030 694 37 31
- 🚇 U-Bahn Gneisenaustrasse

BERLINER ZINNFIGUREN KABINETT

Armies of tin soldiers and herds of miniature farmyard animals are carefully crafted and delicately painted at this shop in Charlottenburg.
- ➕ D7 ✉ Knesebeckstrasse 88
- ☎ 030 313 08 02
- 🚇 S-Bahn Friedrichstrasse

BOOKS IN BERLIN

There is a wide spectrum of English-language books to choose from here, from classical and modern fiction to history, politics, reference and travel.
- ➕ D6 ✉ Goethestrasse
- ☎ 030 313 12 33
- 🚇 S-Bahn Savignyplatz

BUDAPESTER SCHUHE

An impressive selection of designer footwear for men and women with the latest lines from Prada, Dolce & Gabbana, Sergio Rossi, JP Tod's and Miu Miu.
- ➕ D7 ✉ Kurfürstendamm 43
- ☎ 030 88 62 42 06
- 🚇 S-Bahn Savignyplatz

BÜRGEL-HAUS

This shop sells blue-and-cream pottery from the German region of Thüringia at very reasonable prices.
- ➕ J5 ✉ Friedrichstrasse 154
- ☎ 030 204 45 19
- 🚇 U-Bahn Französische Strasse

DNS

New and old vinyl, including the latest techno tracks and some rare oldies.
- ➕ K4 ✉ Alte Schönhauser Strasse 39–40 ☎ 030 247 98 35 🚇 U-Bahn Weinmeisterstrasse

DUSSMANN

This huge book and record store is ideal for last-minute present buying—you could even do all your shopping here. Where CDs are concerned, if they don't have it here, you won't find it anywhere. Stays opens until 10pm.
- ➕ J5 ✉ Friedrichstrasse 90
- ☎ 030 20 25 20 59
- 🚇 S-Bahn Friedrichstrasse

FRITZ

Unique designs by this Berlin based jewellery designer.
- ➕ L7 ✉ Dresdener Strasse 20
- ☎ 030 247 98 35
- 🚇 U-Bahn Kottbusser Tor

GRÜNE PAPETERIE

An environmentally friendly stationers in

Kreuzberg selling stationery, wrapping paper, wooden fountain pens, small gifts and toys.

🚏 L7 ✉ Oranienstrasse 196 ☎ 030 618 53 55 🚇 U-Bahn Kottbusser Tor

HAUS AM CHECKPOINT CHARLIE

The only place in Berlin where you can still find an authentic piece of the Wall; also GDR and Soviet Union medals, military insignia and much more.

🚏 J6 ✉ Friedrichstrasse 43–45 ☎ 030 253 72 50 🚇 U-Bahn Kochstrasse

JOHANNA PETZOLDT

A small shop stacked with traditional hand-made wooden figurines, musical boxes and candle-mobiles from the Erzgebirge region.

🚏 K4 ✉ Sophienstrasse 9 ☎ 030 282 67 54 🚇 S-Bahn Hackescher Markt

KARSTADT SPORT

In the Neues Kranzler Eck this is the largest sports shop in Berlin spread over 6,000m sq (64,580sq ft) on 4 floors. They have everything you could possibly need to help you get in shape.

🚏 E6 ✉ Joachimstaler Strasse 5–6 ☎ 030 88 02 40 🚇 U- or S-Bahn Zoologischer Garten

KULTURKAUFHAUS

This enormous bookstore in the heart of the Mitte has huge stocks of videos, CDs and computer software. There is also a 'cookie café' offering a good selection of cookies based on original American recipes.

🚏 J5 ✉ Friedrichstrasse 90 ☎ 030 20 25 11 11 🚇 U- or S-Bahn Friedrichstrasse

MARGA SCHOELLER

The best selection of fiction and non-fiction books in English in Berlin.

🚏 D7 ✉ Knesebeckstrasse 33–34 ☎ 030 881 11 12 🚇 S-Bahn Savignyplatz

MONDOS ARTS

Memorabilia from the former East Germany including GDR flags and posters, original border signs and various items bearing the Ampelman logo—the little green and red men on the crossing lights in eastern Berlin.

🚏 Off map ✉ Schreinerstrasse 6 ☎ 030 42 01 07 78 🚇 U-Bahn Samariter Strasse

MR DEAD & MRS FREE

This is Berlin's best shop for independent and underground rock.

🚏 G7 ✉ Bülowstrasse 5 ☎ 030 215 14 49 🚇 U-Bahn Nollendorfplatz

ROSSI

Swiss bag designer Francesco Rossi uses high tech materials and retro influences to create his modern functional bags.

🚏 K4 ✉ Alte Schönhauser Strasse 29 ☎ 030 28 04 59 72 🚇 U-Bahn Weinmeisterstrasse

SONY STYLE STORE

On 3 futuristic floors you can hear music, manipulate digital images with Sony Pictures and try out the latest Playstation.

🚏 H6 ✉ Sony Center am Potsdamer Platz ☎ 030 25 75 11 55 🚇 U- or S-Bahn Potsdamer Platz

KURFÜRSTENDAMM

This bustling boulevard in the western heart of Berlin, known as the Ku'damm for short, has a diverse array of shops and is lined with designer boutiques, cafés, theatres, museums, cinemas, art galleries, bars and clubs.

WILMERSDORFERSTRASSE

Between the ICC fairground and the Kurfürstendamm is Wilmersdorferstrasse, affectionately known as 'Wildo' by Berliners. This is one of the oldest and most established shopping streets in the city. As well as department stores you will find plenty of individual boutiques and designer stores along this strip.

Theatres, Concerts & Cinemas

DEUTSCHE STAATSOPER

The handsome neoclassical building dominating Bebelplatz is Berlin's oldest opera house, the Deutsche Staatsoper, built in the reign of Frederick the Great. It is currently engaged in a life-and-death struggle with its chief rival, the Deutsche Oper, for fast-diminishing government subsidies. The roll-call of musicians who have graced this stage is amazing–it includes the composers Mendelssohn, Meyerbeer, Liszt and Richard Strauss, the legendary conductor Wilhelm Furtwängler and, more recently, the pianist Daniel Barenboim.

BERLINER ENSEMBLE

Playwright Bertolt Brecht founded this famous theatre company in 1948, and his plays are still in the repertoire.
J4 ✉ Bertolt-Brecht-Platz ☎ 030 282 31 60 🚇 U-or S-Bahn Friedrichstrasse

CINESTAR IMAX

Berlin's biggest 3-D screen employs the latest technology and electronic glasses to bring you closer to the action.
H6 ✉ Im Sony Center, Potsdamer Strasse 4 ☎ 030 26 06 64 00 🚇 U-Bahn and S-Bahn Potsdamer Platz

DEUTSCHE OPER BERLIN

Opera and modern ballet in an uninspired post-war concert hall.
C6 ✉ Bismarckstrasse 35 ☎ 030 25 00 25 🚇 U-Bahn Deutsche Oper

DEUTSCHE STAATSOPER

Opera and ballet in a beautiful baroque concert hall, now restored after extensive wartime bomb damage.
J5 ✉ Unter den Linden 7 ☎ 030 20 35 40 🚇 U-Bahn Hausvogteiplatz

DEUTSCHES THEATER

The name of theatre director Max Reinhardt was virtually synonymous with the life of this theatre from the turn of 20th the century until the Nazis came to power. Film star Marlene Dietrich performed here.
H4 ✉ Schumannstrasse 13 ☎ 030 25 00 25 🚇 U- or S-Bahn Friedrichstrasse

MAXIM GORKI THEATER

This theatre stages plays by contemporary dramatists and works by classical German playwrights. The Gorki Studio has a more experimental programme.
J5 ✉ Am Festungsgraben 2 ☎ 030 20 22 11 29 🚇 S-Bahn Friedrichstrasse

PHILHARMONIE

One of the world's most famous orchestras, the Berlin Philharmonic, performs in Hans Scharoun's 1960s architectural masterpiece in the Kulturforum. The acoustics are impeccable, tickets as rare as gold dust.
G6 ✉ Herbert-von-Karajan-Strasse ☎ 030 25 48 81 32 🚇 U- or S-Bahn Potsdamer Platz

SCHAUSPIELHAUS BERLIN (KONZERTHAUS)

The magnificent concert hall of the Berlin Symphony Orchestra was designed by architect Karl Friedrich Schinkel in 1818.
J5 ✉ Gendarmenmarkt 2 ☎ 030 25 00 25 🚇 U-Bahn Französische Strasse

THEATER DES WESTENS

Broadway shows.
E6 ✉ Kantstrasse 12 ☎ 01805 60 11 60 🚇 U- or S-Bahn Zoologischer Garten

UFA-FABRIK

A well-known spot for alternative music, dance, film and theatre in Kreuzberg.
Off map to south ✉ Viktoriastrasse 10–18 ☎ 030 75 50 30 🚇 U-Bahn Ullsteinstrasse

Cabaret

BAR JEDER VERNUNFT

Eat, drink and enjoy the show—there's also a piano bar.

🚇 E7 ✉ Schaperstrasse 24 ☎ 030 883 15 82 🚇 U-Bahn Spichernstrasse, Uhlandstrasse

CHAMÄLEON VARIETÉ

Variety at its most expansive in an art-deco setting. Clowns, acrobats, magicians and more; much loved by Berliners.

🚇 K4 ✉ Rosenthaler Strasse 40–41 ☎ 030 282 71 18 🚇 S-Bahn Hackescher Markt

CHEZ NOUS

Famous for its transvestite shows, and still going strong after more than 30 years. You need to reserve well in advance.

🚇 E7 ✉ Marburger Strasse 14 ☎ 030 213 18 10 🚇 U-Bahn Kurfürstendamm

DIE DISTEL

'The Thistle' club is known for its acerbic political satire.

🚇 J5 ✉ Friedrichstrasse 101 ☎ 030 204 47 04 🚇 U- or S-Bahn Friedrichstrasse

FRIEDRICHSTADT-PALAST

The most famous nightspot in eastern Berlin, with a long tradition. In the main revue entertainment includes variety acts, a floor show and loud music; the small revue is more intimate.

🚇 J5 ✉ Friedrichstrasse 107 ☎ 030 23 26 22 03 🚇 U- or S-Bahn Friedrichstrasse

LA VIE EN ROSE

Glamorous showgirls in feathers and pearls sing their hearts out.

🚇 J9 ✉ Tempelhof Airport ☎ 030 69 51 30 00 🚇 U-Bahn Platz der Luftbrücke

KABARETT DIE STACHELSCHWEINE

The political satire here is tame and barely merits the prickly associations in the name (*Stachelschweine* means porcupine).

🚇 E6 ✉ Europa-Center ☎ 030 261 47 95 🚇 U- or S-Bahn Zoologishcher Garten

MEHRINGHOFTHEATER

A Kreuzberg theatre specializing in radical or alternative cabaret.

🚇 J8 ✉ Gneisenaustrasse 2a ☎ 030 691 50 99 🚇 U-Bahn Mehringdamm

POMP, DUCK AND CIRCUMSTANCE

Pomp, Duck and Circumstance is an institution that plays tribute to the glory days of cabaret. During the 4-course meal and 3 and a half hour show you will be treated to a bizarre ensemble of acts—a truly extraordinary and surreal dining experience that is certainly not for the faint hearted.

🚇 H7 ✉ Möckernstrasse 26 ☎ 030 26 94 92 00 🚇 U-Bahn Möckernbrücke

WINTERGARTEN VARIETE

Long synonymous with late-night entertainment, the Wintergarten makes for a fun-packed evening. International variety entertainers star.

🚇 G7 ✉ Potsdamerstrasse 96 ☎ 030 250 08 80 🚇 U-Bahn Kurfürstenstrasse

GOODBYE TO CABARET?

The 1920s was the undisputed golden age of cabaret, a fact seized upon by Bob Fosse in his 1972 film musical *Cabaret*, based on Christopher Isherwood's novel *Goodbye to Berlin*. The main characteristics of the art form—biting political satire and unabashed sexual licence—aroused the wrath of the Nazi ideologues, who closed down the theatres and arrested many of the performers. Since World War II, Berliners have done their best to revive the tradition but the modern clubs are often more like variety shows—the bite is missing.

LANGUAGE PROBLEMS?

Even if you don't speak German, you will probably still enjoy the song and dance element of cabaret shows. However, in order to understand the political satire, some knowledge of the German language and a familiarity with current affairs is needed.

Pubs, Bars & Clubs

LOCAL TIPPLES

A favourite local drink is *Berliner Weisse*, beer with a dash of raspberry or woodruff syrup (*mit Grün*)—addictive if you have a sweet tooth. This is a traditional beverage; more trendy is *Herva mit Mosel*, a peculiar blend of white wine with maté tea that Berliners now consume at least half a million times annually. Hardened drinkers prefer *Korn*, frothy beer with a schnapps chaser.

AMBULANCE

Resident DJs play every night at this small oasis in Mitte. Things hot up after 11pm when the bar fills up with trendy locals and the loungecore, brazilelectro, funk, garage or drum and bass vibes kick in.
🔢 J4 ✉ Oranienburger Strasse 27 ☎ 030 281 20 95 🕐 Mon–Fri from 4pm, Sat–Sun from 6pm. DJs after 10pm 🚇 S-Bahn Hackescher Markt

BAR AM LÜTZOWPLATZ

Cocktail bar with one of the longest happy hours in Berlin (5pm–9pm) and a clientele that likes to see and be seen.
🔢 F6 ✉ Lützowplatz 7 ☎ 030 262 68 07 🕐 Daily 2pm–4am 🚇 U-Bahn Nollendorfplatz

BIG EDEN

Once famous for the international celebrities who used to drop in, Big Eden is now a conventional dance club attracting mainly local 20-somethings.
🔢 D7 ✉ Ku'damm 202 ☎ 030 882 61 20 🕐 Thu from 9pm, Sat, Sun from 11pm 🚇 U-Bahn Uhlandstrasse

EL BARRIO

Popular cellar bar with salsa music. Occasional live bands and salsa classes.
🔢 G7 ✉ Potsdamer Strasse 84 ☎ 030 262 18 52 🕐 Tue–Sun from 10pm, Mon from 9pm 🚇 U-Bahn Kurfürstenstrasse

FAR OUT

A conventional nightclub for the younger crowd, in Berlin's west end. The music tends to be mainstream rock and pop.
🔢 D7 ✉ Ku'damm 156 ☎ 030 32 00 07 17 🕐 Tue 7pm–1am, Wed from 9pm, Thu–Sun from 10pm 🚇 U-Bahn Adenauerplatz

HARRY'S NEW YORK BAR

This piano bar in the Hotel Esplanade attracts a mainly business clientele and is suitably restrained.
🔢 G6 ✉ Im Grand Hotel Esplanade, Lützowufer 15 ☎ 030 254 78 86 33 🕐 Daily noon–4am 🚇 U-Bahn Kurfürstenstrasse

HAVANA

The beat is intoxicating, and so are the Cuba Libres, at this welcoming Latin club in Schöneberg. Choice of three dance floors.
🔢 G8 ✉ Hauptstrasse 30 ☎ 030 784 85 86 🕐 Fri, Sat from 10pm, Wed from 9pm 🚇 U-Bahn Kleistpark

MAXTRIX

Under Warschauer Strasse U-Bahn station, these cave-like rooms with vaulted ceilings dating back to 1901 have been dressed up for the 21st century with plenty of low ultra-violet lighting and neon.
🔢 N7 ✉ Warschauer Platz 18 ☎ 030 29 49 10 47 🕐 Tue, Thu from 9pm, Wed, Sat from 10pm, Fri from 11pm 🚇 U-Bahn Warschauer Strasse

90 GRAD

This popular club can get very crowded in the wee hours. The music veers between hip-hop and techno, with a little soul for good measure.

✚ G7 ✉ Dennewitzstrasse 37
☎ 030 23 00 59 54 ⏰ Fri,
Sat from 11pm Ⓤ U-Bahn
Kurfürstenstrasse

OXYMORON

Busy café-restaurant in
one of the courtyards of
Hackesche Höfe with a
dance club to the rear.
The music is eclectic:
soft rock, drum 'n' bass,
hip-hop and such.
✚ K4 ✉ Rosenthaler Strasse
40–41 ☎ 28391886
⏰ Daily 10pm–4am Ⓢ S-
Bahn Hackescher Markt

PONY BAR

Pony Bar is the brainchild
of a couple of unemployed
architect students. The
bar, in Mitte, creates a
post-modern 1970s/1980s
inspired interior with floral
tablecloths and funky
lamps.
✚ K4 ✉ Alte Schönhauser
Strasse 44 ⏰ Mon–Sat
noon–late, Sun 6–late Ⓤ U-
Bahn Rosa-Luxemburg Platz

ROTE HARFE

One of a crop of lively
modern cafés in
Kreuzberg, the Red Harp
is warm, welcoming and a
touch sophisticated.
✚ L7 ✉ Oranienstrasse 13
☎ 030 618 44 46 ⏰ Daily
9am–late Ⓤ U-Bahn Görlitzer
Bahnhof

SAGE-CLUB

This club in Mitte attracts
a diverse collective of
fashion-conscious clubbers.
Expect to hear everything
from rock, big beat, funk,
soul and house depending
on the night. Long queues
at weekends.
✚ L6 ✉ Köpenicker Strasse
78 ☎ 030 278 98 30 ⏰ Thu
from 10pm, Fri, Sat from 11pm,

Sun from midnight Ⓤ U-Bahn
Görlitzer Bahnhof

STRANDBAR MITTE

It is easy to imagine that
you are by the sea in this
open-air bar on the waters
edge in Mitte. Their beach
parties are the place to be
in the summer. Nice place
to end a morning stroll, too.
✚ K4 ✉ Monbijoustrasse 3
⏰ Daily 10am–late Ⓢ S-
Bahn Hackescher Markt

TRESOR 30

An old favourite that has
stood the test of time.
Berlin techno was born
here.
✚ H6 ✉ Leipziger Strasse
126a ☎ 030 229 04 14
⏰ Wed, Fri, Sat from 11pm
Ⓤ U- or S-Bahn Potsdamer Platz

VICTORIA BAR

A chic retro cocktail bar.
An impressive list of
celebrity DJs and actors
drink here, attracted by
the extensive classic
cocktail menu and quality
service.
✚ H6 ✉ Potsdamer Strasse
102 ☎ 030 25 75 99 77
⏰ Mon–Sun 6pm–3am, happy
hour 6–9 Ⓤ U- or S-Bahn
Potsdamer Platz

ZAPATA

This chilled out café by
day and offbeat bar and
music venue by night is
on the ground floor of the
Tacheles, a former squat
that is now a thriving
cultural base.
✚ J4 ✉ Oranienburger
Strasse 54–56a (Im Kunsthaus
Tacheles ☎ 030 281 61 09
⏰ Daily 10am–late; food
served till 10pm Ⓢ S-Bahn
Hackescher Markt

MUSIC FOR ALL

Musical tastes have splintered
remarkably in recent years; in
Berlin this is reflected by the
plethora of specialist
nightclubs. ebop, house, soul,
jungle, ragga, techno and
heavy metal–pay your money
and take your choice.

Folk, Jazz & Rock

JAZZ FESTIVAL

The annual Berlin Jazz Festival takes place at the beginning of November and lasts just three or four days. The main venue is the Haus der Kulturen der Welt in the Tiergarten. Advance information is available from:
Berliner Festspiele
✉ Budapester Strasse 50
☎ 030 25 48 90

ARENA

An old bus depot in the Treptow district, now a major venue for headline rock and pop bands.
➕ H8 ✉ Eichenstrasse 4
☎ 030 533 73 33 🚇 U-Bahn Schlesisches Tor

A-TRANE JAZZCLUB

This Charlottenburg night haunt caters to lovers of modern jazz and bebop. Concerts usually start at about 10pm.
➕ D7 ✉ Bleibtreustrasse 1
☎ 030 313 25 50 🚉 S-Bahn Savignyplatz

B FLAT

Acoustic music and jazz are on the menu at this long club in the heart of the city. Drinks are cheaper before 10pm and happy hour is between 1am and 2am. There isn't usually an entrance fee.
➕ K4 ✉ Rosenthaler Strasse 13 ☎ 030 283 31 23
🚉 S-Bahn Hackescher Markt

HAUS DER KULTUREN DER WELT

This club regularly hosts rock concerts and showcases African and Latin American music acts.
➕ G5 ✉ John-Foster-Dulles-Allee 10 ☎ 030 39 78 70
🚉 S-Bahn Unter den Linden

KUNSTFABRIK SCHLOT

Three-minutes' walk from Oranienburger Strasse in Mitte this jazz venue has a different live act every day. From Friday to Monday its modern, swing or salsa, Tuesdays and Wednesdays is satire and cabaret and Thursdays is jazz singers night.
➕ H3 ✉ Edisonhöfe,
Chausseestrasse 18 ☎ 030 448 21 60 🚉 S-Bahn Nordbahnhof, U-Bahn Zinnowitzerstrasse

QUASIMODO

Stifling and crowded, this is as good a place as any to hear live jazz, blues and funk. Tickets are available from 3pm on the day of performance. Live music from 10pm.
➕ E6 ✉ Kantstrasse 12a
☎ 030 312 80 86 🚇 U- or S-Bahn Zoologischer Garten

SO 36

Besides the regular weekly programme of club nights—including techno, Asian vibes, 1980s revival, hip hop and house—this club frequently plays host to ska, rock, new metal and punk bands.
➕ L7 ✉ Oranienstrasse 190
☎ 030 61 10 13 13 🕐 Mon from 11pm Electric Ballroom, Wed from 11pm Gay/Lesbian Party, Sun 5pm (summer 7) 🚇 U- or S-Bahn Kottbusser Tor

TRÄNENPALAST

The 'Palace of Tears', the former hall for border and customs procedures is now a well-established concert venue. Rock and pop concerts, discos and cabaret all happen here.
➕ J5 ✉ Reichstagufer 17
☎ 030 206 10 00 🚇 U- or S-Bahn Friedrichstrasse

WALDBÜHNE

Berlin's most famous rock venue, this open-air arena, seating 20,000, regularly hosts some of the world's most prestigious bands and international stars.
➕ Off map ✉ Am Glockenturm
☎ 030 61 10 13 13 🚉 S-Bahn Pichelsberg

Sport

ALBA BERLIN
If you fancy checking out the Albatrosses' skills on the basketball court, head for the Max Schlemming Hall, one of the best sports venues in the world. One mid-week and one weekend match per week all year round
✚ K2 ✉ Cantianstrasse 24 ☎ 030 30 00 90 50 🚇 U-Bahn Eberswalder Strasse

ARS VITALIS
Modern fitness centre with aerobics, weights, sauna and pool. Open to non-members.
✚ F9 ✉ Hauptstrasse 19 ☎ 030 788 35 63 🚇 U-Bahn Rathaus Schöneberg

BERLIN CAPITALS
Ice Hockey is very popular in Germany and a big money game. The Berlin Capitals, or 'The Prussians' as they are more affectionately known, play through the winter at the Eissporthalle in Charlottenburg. Friday or weekend nights from beginning Jan–end Mar
✚ Off map to west ✉ Eissporthalle, Jaffestrasse ☎ 030 30 20 53 91 🚇 S-Bahn Eichkamp

BERLIN THUNDER
The black, red and white players of Berlin Thunder compete in the NFL European League. American football is becoming increasingly popular here. Matches beginning of April until June.
✚ Off map to west ✉ Stadium: Olympiastadion, Olympischer Platz 3 ☎ 030 30 06 44 00 🚇 U-Bahn Olympiastadion

BLUB
Berlin's most famous swimming pool, with indoor and outdoor facilities, boasts Europe's longest 'superslide' (120m/394ft). Sauna and children's play area.
✚ Off map to south ✉ Buschkrugallee 64 ☎ 030 60 90 60 🍴 Restaurant and café 🚇 U-Bahn Grenzallee

FEZ (FREIZEIT-UND-ERHOLUNGSZENTRUM WUHLHEIDE)
A leisure centre in pleasant Köpenick with a swimming pool.
✚ Off map to southeast ✉ Eichgestell, Köpenick ☎ 030 53 07 12 72 🍴 Café 🚇 S-Bahn Wuhlheide

OLYMPIASTADION
This stadium was built to host the 1936 Olympics. Football matches take place here, and the pool is open to the public.
✚ Off map to west ✉ Olympische Platz ☎ 030 30 06 33 🍴 Café 🚇 U-Bahn Olympiastadion (Ost)

STRANDBAD WANNSEE
Wannsee's open-air pool and facilities date from the 1930s but have worn well. Near large beach.
✚ Off map to southwest ✉ Wannseebadweg ☎ 030 803 54 50 🍴 Café 🚇 S-Bahn Nikolassee

TRABRENNBAHN MARIENDORF
Trotting races usually take place on Sundays at this suburban racetrack.
✚ Off map to south ✉ Mariendorfer Damm 222–98 ☎ 030 76 10 01 11 🚇 U-Bahn Alt Mariendorf

CYCLING
Cycling is increasingly popular with Berliners. But beware– cyclists pay scant regard to pedestrians. Bike lights at night, though legally required, seem to be a luxury that many can do without. So, if you hear the frantic ringing of a bell–watch out.

SOCCER
Hertha BSC battled back from bankruptcy in 1994 with the aid of media giant UFA and the team are now battling to stay at the top end of the Bundesleague table. Matches are played every other Saturday during the season

Luxury Hotels

HOTEL PRICES

Expect to pay the following prices per night for a double room, but it's always worth asking when you make your reservation whether any special deals are available.

Luxury	over €180
Moderate	€90–€180
Budget	under €90

HOTEL LOCATIONS

You can stay virtually anywhere in Berlin, but the mid-range hotels tend to cluster around the Ku'damm. Business hotels and luxury hotels tend to be in Mitte. Charlottenburg and Schöneberg are quieter yet equally convenient. The establishments spawned by the East German authorities, such as the Forum on Alexanderplatz, are trying desperately to cope with the chill winds of economic competition. The most scenic locations are Tegel, Wannsee, the Grunewald forest and Müggelsee.

ADLON HOTEL

This historic 337-room hotel, at the Brandenburg Gate is one of the city's most luxurious.
H5 ✉ Unter den Linden 77 ☎ 030 22 61 11 11; www.hotel-adlon.de 🚇 S-Bahn Unter den Linden

BERLIN HILTON

In a great location this hotel has 500 rooms, plus bars, restaurants, fitness centre, pool and fabulous views over the Gendarmenmarkt.
J6 ✉ Mohrenstrasse 30 ☎ 030 20 23 42 55; www.hilton.de 🚇 U-Bahn Stadtmitte

DORINT AM GENDARMENMARKT

Hotel with dark marble and frosted glass in the classy rooms and views of the Gendarmenmarkt.
J6 ✉ Charlottenstrasse 50–52 ☎ 030 20 37 50; www.dorint.de 🚇 U-Bahn Stadtmitte

GRAND HYATT

One of Berlin's newest hotels, the Grand Hyatt has 340 rooms, and a swimming pool and fitness centre with city views.
H6 ✉ Marlene-Dietrich-Platz 2 ☎ 030 25 53 12 34; www.hyatt.com 🚇 U- or S-Bahn Potsdamer Platz

HOTEL BRANDENBURGER HOF

A stylish late 19th-century building, near the Kaiser Wilhelm Memorial Church. Winter garden restaurant and 82 rooms.
E7 ✉ Eislebener Strasse 14 ☎ 030 21 40 50; www.hotel brandenburger-hof.com 🚇 U-Bahn Augsburger Strasse

INTER-CONTINENTAL BERLIN

Berlin's most glamorous hotel has 510 rooms, 70 suites, a swimming pool, sauna and business centre.
F6 ✉ Budapester Strasse 2 ☎ 030 260 02; www.berlin.intercontinetal.com 🚇 U- or S-Bahn Zoologischer Garten

KEMPINSKI HOTEL BRISTOL

Chandeliers and deep carpets recall its resplendent past. Courteous service. 315 rooms, 44 suites, fitness room and swimming pool.
B7 ✉ Ku'damm 27 ☎ 884340; fax 8836075 🚇 U-Bahn Adenauerplatz

MADISON

Zen hotel with peaceful gardens. You will be treated to quality service that is great value for money.
H6 ✉ Potsdamer Platz 3 ☎ 030 590 05 00 00; www.madison-berlin.de 🚇 U- or S-Bahn Potsdamer Platz

SAVOY HOTEL

An elegant hotel with large roof terrace and 125 rooms. A few minutes walk from the Ku'damm.
E7 ✉ Fasanenstrasse 9–10 ☎ 030 31 10 30; www.hotel-savoy.com 🚇 U-Bahn Uhlandstrasse

THE WESTIN GRAND

A five-storey, ultra-modern hotel with 358 rooms, swimming pool and sauna. In Friedrichstrasse.
J5 ✉ Friedrichstrasse 158–164 ☎ www.westin-grand.com 🚇 U- or S-Bahn Friedrichstrasse

Mid-Range Hotels

BERLIN EXCELSIOR HOTEL

Duplex suites, garden terrace, 317 rooms and several restaurants and bars. Well-placed near the Zoo station.

E6 · Hardenbergstrasse 14 · 030 355 22; fax 030 882 55 28 · U- or S-Bahn Zoologischer Garten

BERLIN PLAZA HOTEL

This hotel, near the Ku'damm, has 131 rooms and a terrace restaurant .

D7 · Knesebeckstrasse 63 · 030 88 41 34 44; www.plazahotel.de · U-Bahn Uhlandstrasse

FJORD HOTEL

Clean and modern, this 57-room hotel is convenient for the Kulturforum. Roof terrace open for breakfast in summer.

G7 · Bissingzeile 13 · 030 25 47 20; fax 030 25 47 21 11 · U-Bahn Kurfürstenstrasse

HOTEL ASTORIA

This 32-room hotel is situated among the art galleries of Fasanenstrasse. Bar and baby-sitting service.

E6 · Fasanenstrasse 2 · 030 312 40 67; www.hotelastoria.de · U- or S-Bahn Zoologishcher Garten

HOTEL JURINE

Friendly, family-run hotel close to Prenzlauer Berg. All 49 bright and airy rooms have pay and satellite TV.

K3 · Schwedter Strasse 15 · 030 443 29 90; fax 030 44 32 99 99 · U-Bahn Senefelderplatz

HOTEL RIEHMERS HOFGARTEN

This florid stucco apartment house was built in 1891 for prosperous Berliners. 20 good-sized rooms.

J8 · Yorckstrasse 83 · 30 78 909 88 00; www.riehmers-hofgarten.de · U-Bahn Mehringdamm

HOTEL UNTER DEN LINDEN

A modern hotel with 331 rooms and suites, restaurant, bar and conference facilities.

J5 · Unter den Linden 14 · 030 23 81 10; www.hotel-unter-den-linden.de · U- or S-Bahn Friedrichstrasse

HOTEL VILLA KASTANIA

Comfortable hotel in Charlottenburg. The 44 rooms have good facilities, and there is a pool.

A6 · Kastanienallee 20 · 030 30 00 20; fax 030 30 00 02 10 · U-Bahn Theodor-Heuss-Platz

LA VIE HOTEL JOACHIMSHOF

Comfortable and modern 35-room hotel, opposite the Natural History Museum. Small bar, restaurant and sauna.

H4 · Invalidenstrassse 98 · 030 203 95 61 00; fax 030 203 95 61 99 · U-Bahn Zinnowitzer Strasse

RESIDENZ BERLIN

Jugendstil architecture is one of the boasts of this 80-room hotel near the Ku'damm. Restaurant.

E7 · Meinekestrasse 9 · 030 88 44 30; fax 030 882 47 26 · U-Bahn Kurfürstendamm

HOTEL MEINEKE ARTE

The 60 high-ceilinged rooms of this comfortable hotel are decorated in an old-fashioned bourgeois style, with a modern art touch. A carpeted staircase leads to the first-floor reception desk and the breakfast room is hung with contemporary art. Although this mid-priced hotel is located in the side street of Meinekestrasse, just 200m (220 yards) from the Ku'damm, it's quiet.

030 889 21 20; fax 030 88 67 92 92

Budget Accommodation

WHERE TO LOOK

Berlin offers a surprising variety of lower-priced accommodation and you do not necessarily need to trek out to the backwoods. Schöneberg and Kreuzberg districts both have a plentiful supply of pensions and simple hotels, most of which are clean and up to scratch. Young people may prefer Kreuzberg for its lively night scene.

YOUTH HOSTELS

Youth hostels (*jugendgästehaus* or *jugendherberge*) do not impose restrictions on age or families but to stay in them you do need to be a member of the Youth Hostel Association (YHA). You can buy a membership card from your own national YHA, on arrival at the youth hostel, or from the:

Mitgliederservice des DJH Berlin-Brandenburg
✉ Tempelhofer Ufer 32
☎ 2649520; fax 2640437
You can obtain either a fully valid membership or a guest card with a welcome stamp for each night of your stay. Family membership is also available.

A & O FRIEDRICHSHAIN

Inexpensive rooms in the old east end. Multilingual staff, 30 beds, cut-price meals and bike rental.
➕ Off map to east
✉ Boxhagener Strasse 73
☎ 030 297 78 10; Fax 030 29 00 73 66 🚉 S-Bahn Ostkreuz

BERLINER CITY-PENSION

In the heart of Mitte in Alexanderplatz the rooms in this renovated budget hotel are clean and light.
➕ Off map to east
✉ Proskauer Strasse 13
☎ 030 42 08 16 15;
www.berliner-city-pension.de
🚉 S-Bahn Frankfurter Allee

CIRCUS

City-centre hostel for backpackers. Luggage store, bike rental, ticket service and 24-hour reception.
➕ J4 ✉ Rosa-Luxemburg-Strasse 39–41 ☎ 030 28 39 14 33; www.circus-berlin.de
🚉 U-Bahn Rosenthalerplatz

CITY HOSTEL @HALLESCHES UFER

Great value for money, this stylish hostel has no curfew and a huge breakfast to set you up for the day.
➕ H/J7 ✉ Hallesches Ufer 30
☎ ; www.meininger-hostels.de
🚉 U-Bahn Mendelssohn Bartholdy Platz

FRAUEN HOTEL ARTEMISIA

Just for women—with eight attractive rooms, a bar and a library. In Wilmersdorf. Book early.
➕ C7 ✉ Brandenburgische Strasse 18 ☎ 030 873 89 05;
www.frauenhotel-berlin.de
🚉 U-Bahn Konstanzer Strasse

HOTEL-PENSION AM SCHLOSS BELLEVUE

A family run hotel in a central yet quiet location not far from the Kurfürstendamm.
➕ F4 ✉ Paulstrasse 3
☎ 030 391 12 27 🚉 U-Bahn Turmstrasse

HOTEL TRANSIT LOFT

One of the best hotels in the lower price range, with 47 clean rooms and surprisingly good facilities.
➕ J8 ✉ Greifswalder Strasse 219 ☎ 030 48 49 37 73;
www.hotel-transit.de 🚉 U- or S-Bahn Alexanderplatz

INTERMEZZO–HOTEL FÜR FRAUEN

This small, central, down-to-earth hotel is exclusively for women. Boys up to 12 can stay here too.
➕ H6 ✉ Gertrud-Kolmar-Strasse 5 ☎ 030 22 48 90 96;
www.hotelintermezzo.de 🚉 U- or S-Bahn Potsdamer Platz

LETTE'M SLEEP HOSTEL

This popular youth hostel is a great option for backpackers.
➕ L2 ✉ Lettestrasse 7
☎ 030 447 33 623,
www.backpackers.de
🚉 S-Bahn Prenzlauer Allee

PEGASUS HOSTEL

This hostel has more to offer than most—a garden, excellent cooking facilities, apartments and the choice of private or communal showers.
➕ Off map to east ✉ Strasse der Pariser Kommune 35
☎ 030 29 35 19 10;
www.pegasushostel.de
🚉 S-Bahn Ostbahnhof

BERLIN
travel facts

Essential Facts *90*

Getting Around *91–92*

Communications *92*

Emergencies *92–93*

Language *93*

ESSENTIAL FACTS

Customs regulations
- Duty-free limits for non-EU visitors are: 200 cigarettes or 250g of tobacco or 50 cigars; 2 litres of wine and 1 litre of spirits.

Electricity
- 220 volts on a two-pin plug.

Lavatories
- Men's toilets are labelled *Herren*, women's *Damen* or *Frauen*.
- Public toilets are free but scarce. Use those in cafés, restaurants, hotels and department stores.

Money matters
- Exchange offices (*Wechselstuben*) can be found all over Berlin: Zoo Station (Bahnhof Zoo) 🔟 E6 ⏰ Mon–Sat 7.30–10pm, Sun and holidays 8–7; Friedrichstrasse station 🔟 J5 ⏰ Mon–Fri 7am–7.30pm, Sat–Sun 8–4; holidays 9–2
- Automatic cash dispensers (ATMs) can be found citywide.
- Most major credit cards are recognized but not widely accepted.
- Euro traveller's cheques are preferred, but those in US dollars are acceptable.
- American Express Offices: 🔟 E7 ✉ Uhlandstrasse 173–4 ☎ 030 882 75 75 🔟 J5 ✉ Friedrichstrasse 172 ☎ 030 20 45 57 21

Opening hours
- Shops ⏰ Mon–Fri 9.30–6.30, Sat 9–2. On Thursdays some shops stay open till 8pm
- Banks ⏰ Mon–Fri 9–12.30. Afternoons vary
- Pharmacies ⏰ Mon–Fri 9.30–6.30, Sat 9–2 ☎ 01141 for night pharmacies

Places of worship
- Religious services information: ☎ 01157
- Protestant: Kaiser Wilhelm Memorial Church (▶ 35) ☎ 030 218 50 23. Services ⏰ Sun 10am, 6pm (9am in English during summer)
- Berliner Dom (▶ 47) ☎ 030 20 26 91 11. Services ⏰ Sun 10am, 6pm, (Evensong in English Thu 6pm)
- Roman Catholic: Hedwigskirche (▶ 44) ☎ 030 203 48 10. Masses ⏰ Sun 8am, 10am, noon, 6pm, Sat 7pm
- Anglican: St. George's 🔟 Off map to west ✉ Preussenallee. Holy Communion ⏰ Sun 8am. Morning service ⏰ 10am
- Conservative Jewish: Synagogue Pestalozzistrasse 🔟 D6 ✉ Pestalozzistrasse 14 ☎ 030 313 84 11. Services ⏰ Fri 6pm, Sat 9.30am
- Orthodox Jewish: Adass Jisroel 🔟 J4 ✉ Tucholsky Strasse 40. Services ⏰ Fri 5pm; Sat 9.30am

Public holidays
- 1 January; Good Friday; Easter Monday; 1 May; Ascension Day; Pentecost Monday; 3 October (German Unity Day); Christmas Day; 26 December.

Student travellers
- Special fares from Deutsche Bahn for young people with a *Reisepasse*.
- Discounts on public transport, in museums and some theatres are available with an International Student Identity Card.
- European 'Transalpino' tickets are also available for people under 26.

Tipping
- A service charge is usually included in hotel and restaurant bills. Tip porters, maids and washroom attendants.

Women travellers
- Schokofabrik (Women's Centre): 🔟 L7 ✉ Marianenstrasse 6 ☎ 030 615 24 40 ⏰ Café: Mon–Fri 1pm–midnight, Sun noon–2pm. Turkish bath: Sun–Fri 11–10

GETTING AROUND

- Berlin has an excellent public transport network, with two urban railways and numerous bus and tram routes. The local transport authority is the Berliner Verkehrs-Betriebe (BVG).
- BVG Information Service. Timetables and ticket enquiries ☎ 030 194 49; www.bvg.de
- S-Bahn Berlin GmbH Information Service ☎ 030 29 74 33 33; www.s-bahn-berlin.de

Types of ticket

- The **24-hour ticket** (*Tageskarte*) and the **weekly** *7-Tage-Karte* allow unlimited travel on the BVG network (trains, buses, trams and the ferry from Wannsee to Kladow). The weekly ticket covers unlimited travel during any seven-day period from validation until midnight on the seventh day.
- A **single one-way ticket** (*Einzelfahrausweis*) is valid for two hours. You can transfer or interrupt your travel.
- The *Kurzstrecke* (short-distance ticket) is valid on the U- and S-Bahn for up to three stops including transfers, or for six stops only (bus/tram).
- **BerlinWelcomeCard** entitles one adult and up to three children aged 6–14 to free BVG travel for three days as well as reductions on sightseeing trips, museums and theatres. Enquire at your hotel, tourist information offices or U-Bahn ticket offices.
- Children under 14: reduced-rate travel; children under six: free.

The metro

- The U-Bahn (underground railway) and S-Bahn (city railway), are interchangeable.

- You must buy a ticket from station foyers or from vending machines on platforms. Validate your ticket at a machine on the platform before boarding the train.
- Trains run every five or ten minutes, Mon–Fri 5am–midnight; Sat–Sun (approximately) 4am–2am. On Friday and Saturday there is a round-the-clock service on several city trains and underground lines that runs every 15 minutes.
- You may take bicycles on the U-Bahn on weekdays between 9am and 2pm and after 5.30pm, and all weekend. Cyclists may travel on the S-Bahn at any time. There is a small charge.

Buses

- Central Bus Station, Funkturm ☎ 030 301 80 28
- Pay the driver with small change or show ticket (see above). Multiple tickets, also valid for U- and S-Bahn, can be bought from vending machines at some bus stops or at U-Bahn stations, but not from the driver.
- Route 100 is particularly useful, departing from Zoo Station every 10 minutes and linking the West End with Unter den Linden and Alexanderplatz.
- More than 70 night buses operate half-hourly from 1am to 4am. Line N19 runs through the centre every 15 minutes.

Strassenbahnen

- Trams operate largely in eastern Berlin. Ticket procedures are the same as for buses.

Maps and timetables

- Obtain timetables and maps from large U-Bahn ticket offices such as Alexanderplatz ☎ 030 194 49; www.bvg.de.

Taxis

- Taxis are good value, with stands throughout the city. Only use cabs with a meter.
- There is a small surcharge for baggage.
- Not all drivers know their way, so travel with your own map.
- Central taxi call centre ☎ 0800 800 115 54
- Chauffeur service ☎ 030 213 90 90
- Bike taxis (rickshaws) ☎ 030 44 35 89 90

BVG ferries

- BVG ferry lines in the Wannsee and Köpenick areas include services from Wannsee to Kladow, Glienicker Bridge to Sacrow, Grünau to Wendenschloss and around Müggelsee.

Car sharing

- Visitors can telephone a Mitfahrzentrale (ride centre) to arrange a lift to other German cities in a private car (rates to be agreed beforehand). Mitfahrzentralen are located at: Liebland, U-Bahn Zoo, platform 2 ✚ E6 ☎ 030 194 40 (daily 9am–8pm); U-Bahn Alexanderplatz ✚ K5 ☎ 030 241 58 20 (Mon–Fri 9am–8pm, Sat 10–6, Sun 11–4); U- or S-Bahn Yorckstrasse ✚ H8 ☎ 030 216 40 20 (Mon–Fri 9am–8pm, Sat, Sun 10–6)

COMMUNICATIONS

Telephones

- In phone boxes marked *Kartentelefon* use phone cards, available from post offices, petrol stations and newspaper kiosks.
- Boxes marked *International* and telephones in post offices are for long-distance calls.
- Calls are cheapest after 10pm and on Sundays.
- Follow the dialling instructions (in several languages) in the box.
- To call the UK from Berlin dial 0044, then omit the first 0 from the area code.
- To call Berlin from the UK dial 0049 30, then the number.
- To call the US from Berlin dial 001. To call Berlin from the US dial 01149 30, then the number.
- Local operator 03; international 0010.

Post offices

- Open: 🕐 Mon–Fri 8–6, Sat 8–noon
- Poste restante (*postlagernde Sendungen*): Joachimsthaler Strasse 7 🕐 Mon–Sat 8am–midnight, Sun 10am–midnight ☎ 0180 233 33
- US citizens can receive mail at the American Express Office ✉ Ku'damm 11 ☎ 030 882 75 75
- Other post offices: ✉ Alte Potsdamer Strasse 7 🕐 Mon–Fri 9am–8pm, Sat 9am–4pm; ✉ Nürnberger Strasse 8 🕐 Mon–Fri 8am–6pm, Sat 8am–1pm
- Stamps can be bought from vending machines on the Ku'damm, as well as from post offices.
- Postboxes are bright yellow.

EMERGENCIES

Sensible precautions

- Although Berlin is one of the safer European cities, always remain on your guard. Keep a close eye on bags and do not hang them on the back of chairs in restaurants.
- Avoid poorly lit areas, some places such as Oranienburger Strasse can become seedy red-light districts at night.
- Thieves often target tourists on on the U-Bahn and trams so keep wallets and purses concealed when travelling on them.
- Bicycle theft is common.

Lost property

- Police, Tempelhof ✚ J9
  ✉ Platz der Luftbrücke 6 ☎ 6995
- BVG Transport Lost and Found
  ☎ 25623040

Medical and dental treatment

- There are plenty of English-speaking doctors in Berlin. For a referral service telephone the medical emergency number.
- Emergency numbers:
  Medical ☎ 31 00 31
  Dental ☎ 89 00 43 33
  Poison ☎ 030 192 40

Medicines

- Take any specially prescribed medications with you. Check on the generic name of any drugs before you leave home.

Emergency phone numbers

- Coins are not needed for emergency calls from public telephones: Police ☎ 110; Fire ☎ 112; Ambulance ☎ 115
- American Hotline: crisis hotline and free, recorded medical referral service ☎ 0177 8141510

Embassies in Berlin

- UK ✉ Unter den Linden 32–34 ☎ 030 20 18 40
- US ✉ Neustädtischer Kirchstrasse 4–5 ☎ 030 238 51 74

Tourist information offices

- Tourist Info Center, Europa-Center ✚ E6 ✉ Budapester Strasse 45 🕒 Mon–Sat 10–7, Sun 10–6 🚉 S- or U-Bahn Zoologischer Garten
- Tourist Info Café Unter den Fernsehturm ✉ Alexanderplatz 🕒 Daily 10–6 🚉 S- or U-Bahn Alexanderplatz
- Brandenburg Gate 🕒 Daily 10–6 🚉 S- or U-Bahn Unter den Linden
- Berlin Tourismus Marketing GmbH (office) ✉ Am Karlsbad 11 ☎ 030 25 00 25; www.berlin-tourist-information.de

LANGUAGE

yes ja
no nein
please bitte
thank you danke
good morning guten Morgen
good evening guten Abend
good night gute Nacht
goodbye auf Wiedersehen
today heute
yesterday gestern
tomorrow morgen
small klein
large gross
quickly schnell
cold kalt
hot warm
good gut
menu die Speisekarte
breakfast das Frühstück
lunch das Mittagessen
dinner das Abendessen
white wine der Weisswein
red wine der Rotwein
beer das Bier
bread das Brot
milk die Milch
sugar der Zucker
water das Wasser
bill die Rechnung
room das Zimmer
open offen
closed geschlossen
how much? wieviel?
expensive teuer
cheap billig
do you speak English? sprechen Sie Englisch?
I don't speak German Ich spreche kein Deutsch
I don't understand Ich verstehe nicht
Excuse me Entschuldigen Sie
train station der Bahnhof
airport der Flughafen
bank die Bank
post office das Postamt
police die Polizei
hospital das Krankenhaus

93

Index

A

arriving in Berlin 6
accommodation 86–88
Ägyptisches Museum 52
airports 6
Alexanderplatz 49
Applied Art, Museum of
   38, 50

B

Babelsberg Film Studio
   61
Bauhaus-Archiv 36
Bauhaus Museum 36
Berggruen Collection 54
Berlin Cathedral 47
Berliner Dom 47
Berlin Film Museum 40
Berlin Hi-Flyer 59
Berlin Wall 16, 42
Berliner Schloss 47
Blub-Badeparadies 61
boat tours 20
Bode-Museum 45
Botanical Garden 58
Botanischer Garten 58
Brandenburg 21
Brandenburg Gate 41
Brandenburger Tor 41
Breitscheidplatz 35
bridges 56
Britzer Garten 58
Bröhan Museum 52
Brücke Museum 54
buses and trams 7, 91

C

cabaret 81
cafés 70–71
Cecilienhof, Schloss 27
Charlottenburg,
   Schloss 33, 76
Checkpoint Charlie 42
children's activities 61
City Hall 49
city tours 20
climate 4
credit cards 90
crime 92–93
currency 6, 90
customs regulations 90
cycling 62, 85

D

Deutsche Staatsoper 44,
   80
Deutscher Dom 43

Deutsches Historisches
   Museum 44
Deutsches Technik-
   museum 53, 61
disabilities, visitors with 7
driving 7

E

Eastside Gallery 54
Egyptian Museum 52
electricity 90
embassies 93
emergencies 92–93
Ephraim-Palais 48
Ethnological Museum 32
Ethnologisches Museum
   32
Europa-Center 79
events 4, 84
excursions 20–21

F

Fernsehturm 49
ferry services 92
Filmmuseum Berlin 53
folk, jazz and rock 84
food and drink
   bars 82–83
   cafés 34, 70–71
   eating out 64–71
   food shops 77
Französischer Dom 43
Freizeitpark Tegel 58
Friedrichs-Brücke 56
Friedrichwerdersche
   Kirche 55
Funkturm 59
furnishings 76

G

galleries, commercial 75
Gedenkstätte Deutscher
   Widerstand 62
Gedenkstätte Haus der
   Wannsee Konferenz
   57
Gemäldegalerie 37
Gendarmenmarkt 43
German History
   Museum 44
German Resistance,
   Memorial to 60
German Technology
   Museum 52, 61
Gertraudenbrücke 56
Gethsemane Kirche 55
Glienicker Brücke 28

Globe Fountain 35
'Gold Else' 39
Grunewald 30
Grunewaldsee 30
Grunewaldturm 30

H

Hamburger Bahnhof 54
Haus der Kulturen der
   Welt 60
Hedwigskirche 44
history 16–17
Hitler, Adolf 17, 60
home furnishings 76
hotels 86–88
Huguenot Museum 43
Humboldt University 44
hunting museum 30

I

Iduna House 34
Indian & East Asian Art,
   Museums of 53

J

Jagdschloss Grunewald 30
jazz festival 84
jazz venues 84
Jewish Museum 53
Jüdisches Museum 53
Jungfernbrücke 56

K

Kaiser-Wilhelm-
   Gedächtniskirche 35
Kaiser Wilhelm
   Memorial Church 35
Käthe-Kollwitz-
   Museum 34
Klein-Glienicke,
   Schloss 28
Kleistgrab 60
Kleist's Grave 60
Klosterhof 28
Knoblauchhaus 48
Königliche Porzellan
   Manufaktor
   (KPM) 76
Konzerthaus 43
Köpenick, Schloss 50
Kronprinzenpalais 44
Krumme Lanke 30
Kulturforum 37
Kunstgewerbemuseum
   38, 50
Kupferstich-Kabinett 54
Kurfürstendamm 34, 79

L

Langes Luch 30
language 93
lavatories 90
Lessingbrücke 56
Literaturhaus 34
live music 84
lost property 93
Lübbenau 21
Lustgarten 47
Lutherhaus 20
Lutherstadt
 Wittenberg 20
Luxemburg, Rosa 39, 56

M

Marienkirche 49
markets 19, 77
Märkisches Museum 53
Marmorpalais 27
Marx and Engels
 (sculptures) 60
Mauerpark 62
medical treatment 93
medicines 93
metro 7, 91
Moabiter Brücke 56
Moltkebrücke 56
Monbijou Park 61
money 6, 90
monuments 60
Moore, Henry
 (sculpture) 60
Müggelturm 59
Museum für Indische
 Kunst; Ostasiatische
 Kunst 53
Museum Für
 Naturkunde 53
Museumsinsel 45
Museums Island 45
Musical Instruments,
 Museum of 37

N

Napoleon 16
Natural History Museum
 53
Neue Nationalgalerie 37
Neue Synagoge 55
Neue Wache 44
New National Gallery 37
New Palace 26
New Synagogue 55
nightclubs 82–83
Nikolaikirche 48
Nikolaiviertel 48

O

Oberbaumbrücke 56
Old Royal Library 44
Olympiastadion 59, 85
Olympic Stadium 59, 85
opening hours 90

P

Panorama 59
Pariser Platz 41
parks and gardens 58
passports and visas 6
Pergamon Museum 46
places of worship 55, 90
population 15
porcelain 76
post offices 92
Potsdam Conference 27
Potsdamer Platz 40
Prenzlauer Berg 10, 18, 22
public holidays 90
public transport 6–7,
 91–92
pubs and bars 82–83

Q

Quadriga 41

R

Reichstag 57
Rotes Rathaus 49

S

Sachsenhausen 31
Sanssouci, Schloss 26
Sammlung Berggruen 54
Sammlung Industriele
 Gestlang 53
Schiller monument 60
Schinkel, K. F. 28, 33, 41,
 43, 44, 45, 55, 56, 58
Schleusenbrücke 56
Schloss Glienicke 28
Schlossbrücke 56
Schlossinsel 50
Schöneberg 10, 23
Sealife Berlin 61
sensible precautions 92
shopping 18–19, 72–79
Siegessäule 39
Sophienkirche 55
Soviet War Memorial 60
Sowjetisches Ehrenmal 60
Spandau Zitadelle 29
sport 85
Sony Center 40
souvenirs 72

statues 60
Story of Berlin 53
student travellers 90

T

taxis 92
telephone numbers,
 emergency 92–93
telephones 92
theatres and concerts 80
Tiergarten 13, 39
Tierpark Berlin-
 Friedrichsfelde 58
time differences 4
Topographie des Terrors
 57
Topography of Terror 57
tourist offices 93
train services 7, 91
traveller's cheques 90
travelling to Berlin 6–7
Treptower Park 58

U

Unter den Linden 44

V

views 59
Viktoriapark 58
Villa Grisebach 34
Volkspark
 Jungfernheide 58

W

walks 22–23
Wannsee Conference
 Centre 57
Wannsee-Kladow ferry
 62
Wars of Liberation,
 Monument to the 58
Wilhelm II, Kaiser 16, 27,
 30, 35
Wilmersdorferstrasse 79
Winterfeldtplatz 19, 77
Wittenbergplatz
 U-Bahn 62
women travellers 90

Z

Zeiss-Gross-Planetarium
 61
Zeughaus 44
Zitadelle 29
Zoo and Aquarium 61
Zoologischer Garten 61
Zum Nussbaum 48, 71

CityPack
Berlin *Top 25*

ABOUT THE AUTHORS
Christopher Rice writes regularly on Eastern Europe and Russia and holds a PhD from the Centre for Russian and East European Studies at Birmingham University. His wife, Melanie, is also a writer and shares his fascination with this part of the world. The Rices have written a number of guidebooks including *Berlin* in the AA/Thomas Cook series.

Authors *Christopher and Melanie Rice* **Edition Reviser** *Nicola Lancaster*
Managing Editors *Apostrophe S Limited* **Cover Design** *Tigist Getachew, Fabrizio La Rocca*

A CIP catalogue record for this book is available from the British Library.

ISBN-10: 0 7495 4352 3
ISBN-13: 978 0 7495 4352 5

Published by AA Publishing, a trading name of Automobile Association Developments Limited, whose registered office is Southwood East, Apollo Rise, Farnborough, Hampshire, GU14 0JW. Registered number 1878835.

© **AUTOMOBILE ASSOCIATION DEVELOPMENTS LIMITED** 1996, 1999, 2002, 2005
First published 1996, Revised third edition 2002. Reprinted Mar and Oct 2000.
Reprinted Feb and Dec 2003. Reprinted Jul 2004. Revised fourth edition 2005.

Colour separation by Keenes, Andover
Printed and bound by Hang Tai D&P Limited, Hong Kong

ACKNOWLEDGEMENTS
The Automobile Association would like to thank the following photographers, libraries and agencies for their assistance in the preparation of this title.
Illustrated London News 16c; **Stockbyte** 5; **World Pictures** 42
The remaining photographs are held in the Association's own library (AA WORLD TRAVEL LIBRARY) with contributions from the following:
Adrian Baker 16/17, 23, 34, 50t, 50b, 53; **Pete Bennett** 21; **Simon McBride** 8cl, 8bl, 8c, 8b, 8/9, 9cr, 9c, 10c, 11, 12c, 12/13, 15l, 15r, 18c, 18/19, 19c, 19r, 24r, 25, 40t, 57, 63b, 89t; **Clive Sawyer** 22b, 26, 27t, 27b, 28, 29t, 29b, 31t, 31b, 37, 41b, 43t, 47t, 48, 49b, 56, 60; **Jonathon Smith** 1b, 9t, 9b, 10t, 12t, 13, 14t, 14b, 16t, 18t, 20t, 22t, 24t, 24l, 40c, 51t, 54, 59; **Tony Souter** 1t, 2, 4, 6, 17, 30, 32t, 32b, 33t, 33b, 35t, 35b, 36, 38t, 38b, 39t, 39b, 41t, 43b, 44, 45, 46, 47b, 49t, 51b, 52, 55, 58, 61, 62, 63t; **Doug Traverso** 20c, 89b

A01992
Fold out map © Mairs Geographischer Verlag / Falk Verlag, 73751 Ostfildern, Germany
Transport map © TCS, Aldershot, England

TITLES IN THE CITYPACK SERIES
• Amsterdam • Bangkok • Barcelona • Beijing • Berlin • Boston • Brussels & Bruges • Chicago • Dublin •
• Florence • Hong Kong • Lisbon • London • Los Angeles • Madrid • Melbourne • Miami • Milan •
• Montréal • Munich • Naples • New York • Paris • Prague • Rome • San Francisco • Seattle • Shanghai •
• Singapore • Sydney • Tokyo • Toronto • Venice • Vienna • Washington DC •